Fatal Encounter

A thriller

Francis Durbridge

Samuel French — London
New York - Toronto - Hollywood

© 2002 by N. E. Durbridge, Trading as Serial Productions

Rights of Performance by Amateurs are controlled by Samuel French Ltd, 52 Fitzroy Street, London W1T 5JR, and they, or their authorized agents, issue licences to amateurs on payment of a fee. **It is an infringement of the Copyright to give any performance or public reading of the play before the fee has been paid and the licence issued.**

The Royalty Fee indicated below is subject to contract and subject to variation at the sole discretion of Samuel French Ltd.

Basic fee for each and every
performance by amateurs   Code M
in the British Isles

The Professional Rights are controlled by The Agency (London) Ltd, 24 Pottery Lane, Holland Park, London, W11 4LZ.

The publication of this play does not imply that it is necessarily available for performance by amateurs or professionals, either in the British Isles or Overseas. Amateurs and professionals considering a production are strongly advised in their own interests to apply to the appropriate agents for written consent before starting rehearsals or booking a theatre or hall.

ISBN 0 573 01962 2

Please see page iv for further copyright information.

CHARACTERS

Howard Mansfield
Grace Kingsley
Joanna Mansfield
Mark Adler
Perry Kingsley
Chris Coldwell
Rex Winter
Hilary van Zale

SYNOPSIS OF SCENES

The action takes place in the living-room of Howard Mansfield's large house in Holland Park, London

ACT I SCENE 1. An afternoon in July
       SCENE 2. Later that day
       SCENE 3. Three hours later
       SCENE 4. The next morning
       SCENE 5. Early evening, the same day

ACT II SCENE 1. Immediately following
       SCENE 2. Two hours later
       SCENE 3. An hour later
       SCENE 4. The following morning
       SCENE 5. Several hours later

Time —the present

COPYRIGHT INFORMATION

(See also page ii)

This play is fully protected under the Copyright Laws of the British Commonwealth of Nations, the United States of America and all countries of the Berne and Universal Copyright Conventions.

All rights including Stage, Motion Picture, Radio, Television, Public Reading, and Translation into Foreign Languages, are strictly reserved.

No part of this publication may lawfully be reproduced in ANY form or by any means — photocopying, typescript, recording (including video-recording), manuscript, electronic, mechanical, or otherwise—or be transmitted or stored in a retrieval system, without prior permission.

Licences for amateur performances are issued subject to the understanding that it shall be made clear in all advertising matter that the audience will witness an amateur performance; that the names of the authors of the plays shall be included on all programmes; and that the integrity of the authors' work will be preserved.

The Royalty Fee is subject to contract and subject to variation at the sole discretion of Samuel French Ltd.

In Theatres or Halls seating Four Hundred or more the fee will be subject to negotiation.

In Territories Overseas the fee quoted above may not apply. A fee will be quoted on application to our local authorized agent, or if there is no such agent, on application to Samuel French Ltd, London.

VIDEO-RECORDING OF AMATEUR PRODUCTIONS

Please note that the copyright laws governing video-recording are extremely complex and that it should not be assumed that any play may be video-recorded for whatever purpose without first obtaining the permission of the appropriate agents. The fact that a play is published by Samuel French Ltd does not indicate that video rights are available or that Samuel French Ltd controls such rights.

*Other plays by Francis Durbridge
published by Samuel French Ltd:*

Deadly Nightcap
The Gentle Hook
House Guest
Murder With Love
The Small Hours
Suddenly at Home
Sweet Revenge
A Touch of Danger

ACT I

Scene 1

The living-room of a large house in Holland Park, London. An afternoon in July

The house belongs to Howard Mansfield, a well-known book publisher, and this room reflects his good taste and numerous interests. There is an impressive collection of books and pictures. One of the pictures has the title "Flowers On A Tray". There are armchairs; tables; a comfortable sofa; drinks cabinet, including a bottle of Scotch and glasses; and several occasional pieces. There is a window that opens on to the garden. A desk with drawers and a built-in-cupboard stands in front of the window. On the desk is a telephone and a large stiletto-type letter opener. Various letters, etc, are strewn across the desk. UC, *there is a small alcove complete with a table and a couple of chairs. This was originally used for breakfast but books and manuscripts have taken over. There are doors to a conservatory and dining-room. The front door of the house is reached off stage through a furnished hallway. A staircase, only partly visible, leads out of the hallway to the upper part of the house*

When the CURTAIN *rises, Howard is sitting at his desk, dictating a letter to his secretary, Hilary van Zale. He is replying to a letter he is holding*

Howard (*dictating*) ... I can only suggest that you read the contract again, paying attention to Clause 5a. This clause was inserted, at your request, in order to clarify the position with regard to this particular book. I'm afraid there is nothing more I can add ... Yours sincerely ... (*He hands the letter to Hilary*)

Hilary rises, and gathers up the other letters and papers

Hilary I'll type these tonight and get them off tomorrow morning.
Howard Thank you. (*He stretches his arms*) I must say I envy you, Hilary. I wouldn't mind a few days in the South of France myself, at the moment. When are you off?
Hilary We're not.
Howard (*with surprise*) You're not?

Hilary No, my conscientious husband has suddenly decided we should spend the next couple of weeks in his constituency.
Howard Oh, dear! That's not much of a holiday for you.
Hilary I know, but it can't be helped. Roger's got a bee in his bonnet at the moment. At all costs, he mustn't neglect his constituents.
Howard What about you?
Hilary Wives don't count.
Howard I should try and talk him out of it, if I were you.
Hilary I shouldn't have married an MP. You did warn me.

The doorbell rings

Howard That'll be Grace. I'm expecting her. Would you let her in, Hilary.
Hilary I'll ring you before we go up North.
Howard Yes, please do.

Hilary exits

Howard tidies his desk

Grace Kingsley enters. She is carrying a bulky looking manuscript

Hallo, Grace! Good of you to drop in. (*He finishes at the desk and moves down to Grace, indicating the manuscript. Curiously*) Well? Have you read it?
Grace Yes, I've read it. And I like it.
Howard (*with astonishment*) You do!
Grace I loved it. Every word of it. And if you've got any sense you'll go ahead and publish.
Howard My dear, if you like it, of course we'll publish! No argument! Look what happened to "Candle to the Devil". Top of the bestsellers for twenty weeks — and we all hated it! Every one of us, except you.
Grace Well — this is better than "Candle to the Devil". Take my word for it. (*She crosses the room and puts the manuscript down on the desk*)
Howard Someone told me they saw that ex-husband of yours the other day, Grace.
Grace It's possible. He's over here.
Howard What's Perry doing in London?
Grace Can't you guess?
Howard (*as a sudden thought*) Don't tell me! That café-cum-take-away of his finally went bust?
Grace That's about it. Although he doesn't put it that way. He simply says he woke up one morning, discovered he hated Ibiza, gave away the take-away, and caught the next plane to Gatwick.

Act I, Scene 1   3

Howard That figures. How long did he have the café? Can't have been more than a year.
Grace A little longer, maybe.
Howard That's good going for Perry. Did you ever see the place?
Grace No, I've never been to Ibiza. I was invited to the opening but I didn't go. He's now talking of starting an antiques business in Milton Cross.
Howard What on earth does Perry know about antiques?
Grace I can't imagine. I'm the only antique he's ever had — and he never discovered how old I was!
Howard Did he tell you what he's using for money these days?
Grace No. He didn't. But he seems to have plenty of it. He's bought himself a Mercedes.
Howard (*shaking his head*) How an intelligent woman like you keeps falling for that wheeler-dealer, I'll never know.
Grace That's a little unkind, Howard.
Howard Where's he staying, do you know?
Grace He's rented a flat in Pimlico. (*She moves down to Howard*) Joanna's out, I take it?
Howard Yes, she's at the hairdresser's.
Grace I gather she still hasn't got her licence back?
Howard No, but she hasn't long to go.
Grace My goodness, it must have been frustrating for her. (*Amused*) But I ask you, eighty miles an hour in a built up area!
Howard Eighty-five miles an hour!
Grace If that wasn't asking for trouble!
Howard Yes, well — let's hope she's been taught a lesson. But I doubt it. The squabbles we've had over her driving! You just wouldn't believe it, Grace! And in the end of course ——
Grace She always had her own way?
Howard (*lightly*) Always ... (*Pause*) Have you seen Joanna recently?
Grace We had lunch together last week.
Howard Oh! She never told me. How do you think she's looking?
Grace Since you ask me, I didn't think she was her usual self, and she drank too much.

Howard gives an understanding little nod

Howard Did she tell you we're thinking of selling the cottage?
Grace No, she didn't! That does surprise me.
Howard Joanna never wants to go down to Sutton Valence. In fact, she's taken a positive dislike to the place.
Grace But she adores Kent! Surely, that's why you bought the cottage in the first place? (*With concern*) What's the matter with her, Howard? Isn't she well?

Howard I honestly don't know, Grace.
Grace Whenever we meet these days she seems distracted. As if something's worrying her. We used to have a great deal to say to each other. But — last week, for instance — she wasn't a bit interested in anything I had to say.
Howard I know only too well what you mean.
Grace How long has she been like this?
Howard About three weeks. It started one Sunday. We were staying at the cottage and she suddenly decided to go for a walk. I didn't go with her because I had a book I wanted to finish. She was away about half an hour and when she returned she was in a terrible state; practically in tears. For a while I couldn't get any sense out of her. Then, after she'd had a drink, she told me what happened. About ten minutes or so after leaving the cottage, a man appeared with a dog. The dog wasn't on a leash and it went for Joanna. The man finally restrained the animal, but only after it had scared the life out of her. So much so, in fact, she ran all the way back to the cottage.
Grace Was she hurt, physically?
Howard No.

Pause

Grace And this happened three weeks ago?
Howard Yes.
Grace (*after consideration*) Surely, she should have got over it by now?
Howard I would have thought so.

Grace gazes at him, a shade hesitant

Grace Did you believe her story?
Howard At first, yes. Completely. But later, I began to have doubts.
Grace Why? (*With curiosity*) Why was that?
Howard When she first described the incident she was sure the dog was a Rottweiler. But a couple of days later when I questioned her, she said it was an Alsatian. On top of which, she contradicted pretty well everything else she'd told me. (*A brief, awkward silence*) But that's not the whole story, I'm afraid.
Grace No?
Howard No. The night before last we were due to go to the theatre. Joanna wasn't at all keen and at the last minute she said she had a headache and cried off. I had to go. The play was by one of our authors. Anyway, the play was a terrible bore and I escaped as quickly as I could. My car was parked by Covent Garden and just before I turned into Mercer Street a taxi raced by. A woman was in the cab. She was sitting on her own and I saw her quite clearly. It was Joanna.

Act I, Scene 1

Grace (*with astonishment*) Joanna?
Howard Yes.
Grace Did she see you?
Howard I don't think so. In fact, I'm sure she didn't.
Grace (*nonplussed*) Are you certain it was Joanna? Absolutely certain?
Howard I'm positive, Grace. However — when I arrived home she was in bed, apparently asleep. The next morning she told me that she'd gone to bed early and taken a sleeping pill.
Grace Did you mention the taxi? Did you tell her that you'd seen her?
Howard No.
Grace Why not?

Howard hesitates

Why not, Howard?
Howard (*inexorably*) Because I suddenly realized that if she was having an affair with someone ——
Grace (*stopping him with almost a note of ridicule in her voice*) Joanna's not having an affair! Put that ridiculous thought out of your head! I'm her best friend, Howard. If there was anything like that going on, I'd know about it, believe me.
Howard Then what the devil is going on? She was in that cab, Grace! I know she was! And she lied about the dog, I'm sure of that now!
Grace (*shaking her head*) I don't know what's going on. Like you, I haven't the faintest idea. But I'll certainly try and find out. Now stop worrying. (*She moves towards the hall*)
Howard (*as Grace moves*) I've got this wretched dinner tonight.
Grace The booksellers' jamboree?
Howard That's right. Are you going?
Grace No. I went last year and I've never been so bored in my life. I couldn't have gone anyway. I'm staying the night with some friends of mine in Hertfordshire.
Howard (*anxiously*) You'll be back in time for the Board meeting tomorrow afternoon?
Grace Good heavens, yes!
Howard That's most important. It could well be a difficult meeting. We shall be discussing the American offer. I shall need all the support I can get.
Grace Don't worry, I'll be there. Three o'clock?

Grace gives a friendly wave and exits

Howard crosses to the desk and looks at the manuscript. He turns over the pages

Grace returns. She is now holding a large, expensive looking handbag

Howard ...

Howard turns

I found this handbag. It was outside the front door.
Howard (*puzzled*) Outside the door?
Grace Yes. It looks like Joanna's to me.
Howard (*joining her*) What the devil was it doing there?
Grace I don't know. It certainly wasn't there when I arrived.

Howard takes the bag from Grace and examines it

Is it Joanna's?
Howard (*thoughtfully*) Yes. I gave it to her the Christmas before last.

Pause

Grace (*not very convincingly*) She must have left it somewhere. Most probably at the hairdresser's.
Howard And they returned it?

Grace nods

Leaving it outside the front door?

Grace thinks for a moment

Grace That doesn't make sense, does it?
Howard (*quietly*) No. It certainly doesn't.

They stand for a moment looking at each other, both obviously puzzled

Grace Anyway — at least she hasn't lost it.

Howard is staring at the bag again

I daresay there's a simple explanation.
Howard (*curiously*) I'll be interested to hear it.

Pause

Act I, Scene 1   7

Grace Let me know what Joanna's got to say about it.
Howard (*his thoughts elsewhere*) Yes, I'll do that. Thank you, Grace.

Grace looks as if she wishes to continue the conversation, then, changing her mind, she exits

Howard takes the handbag down to the desk, opens it, and proceeds to examine the contents. The bag reveals a wallet, a bunch of keys, a number of credit cards, a bank statement, and what would appear to be a small torch. This is, in fact, a personal alarm system. He accidentally sets off the alarm and it takes several seconds before he is able to stop the siren. Having done this, he turns his attention to the bank statement. It is obvious that he is both surprised and puzzled by what he reads. He studies the statement for a little while before finally picking up the telephone. He dials

(*Into the phone*) Nat West? This is Howard Mansfield. ... I'd like to speak to Mr Selkirk. ... Yes, I'll hold. (*Pause*) ... George? Howard. ... George, Joanna's got a query, perhaps you could sort it out for her? (*He looks at the statement*) On her last statement there's a credit for fifteen thousand pounds and she can't recall what it was for, or where it came from. ... Yes, a credit. ... July, fourth. ... (*An appreciable pause*) ... It was what? A transfer from her deposit account. ... Thank you, George. (*He replaces the receiver and looks at the bank statement with renewed interest*)

The front doorbell rings loudly and unexpectedly

Howard freezes

Pause

The doorbell rings for a second time and continues ringing

Howard reaches a decision. He gathers up the various articles, puts them back in the handbag and places the bag in the cupboard of the desk

   Howard hurries out into the hall

Pause

There is the sound of the front door opening, immediately followed by the sound of voices

Howard (*off: alarmed*) Joanna! What is it? What's happened?

Mark (*off*) I'm afraid you wife's had a very nasty experience, Mr Mansfield.
Howard (*off*) What's the matter, Joanna? Are you ill?
Joanna (*off; on edge*) No! No, I'm all right! Please don't fuss, Howard! Do come along in, Mr Adler.

Joanna Mansfield enters. She has recently been the victim of an attack and, although not injured, she is certainly suffering from the after-effects of the incident. She is followed by her husband and Mark. Mark, a rather distinguished looking man, is carrying a dress-shop carrier belonging to Joanna

Mark Your wife was mugged, Mr Mansfield ...
Howard My God! (*He takes hold of Joanna, concerned*) Are you all right, Joanna? Shall I call the doctor?
Joanna No! No, please don't do that!
Howard Are you sure?
Joanna Yes, I'm quite sure. (*She releases herself from Howard's hold*) Now please, don't fuss, Howard. I'm home now, thanks to Mr Adler. And I'm feeling better already.

Howard looks at Mark and thinks he recognizes him

Howard What happened, Joanna?
Joanna A man stole my handbag ... While we were struggling I had a blackout and Mr Adler came to my rescue. (*To Mark*) I don't know what to say to you. I really don't! You've been terribly kind.

Mark smiles and puts the carrier down on one of the chairs

Mark If I were you, Mrs Mansfield, I'd take things easy for the next couple of hours.
Joanna That's exactly what I've got in mind. And thank you again, Mr Adler.
Mark I hope you'll soon feel better. I'm sure you will.

Joanna exits into the conservatory

Howard is about to follow Joanna when Mark nods to Howard to indicate he is about to take his leave

Howard Please! Don't go Mr — Adler, did my wife say?
Mark Yes.
Howard You're not Mark Adler, by any chance? The art dealer?

Act I, Scene 1   9

Mark Yes, I'm Mark Adler.
Howard I thought I recognized you. Please, don't go! I'd very much like to have a word with you. I won't keep you a minute. (*He picks up the carrier*)

Howard exits into the conservatory

Mark, almost immediately, starts taking an interest in the room. He looks at an attractive painting — "Flowers On A Tray"

Howard returns

Mark (*turning*) This is very good, Mr Mansfield. Did you buy it from a gallery?
Howard No. I bought it privately.
Mark (*looking at the picture again*) "Flowers On A Tray" — a very attractive picture. (*Moving to Howard*) Is there something you wanted to ask me?
Howard Yes, there is. But first — it was most kind of you to look after my wife. I appreciate it.
Mark It was the least I could do under the circumstances.
Howard What happened this afternoon? I'd very much like to hear your version of what took place.

Mark looks at him, sensing the apparent importance Howard attaches to the question

Mark There's very little to tell. I was parking my car on a meter near Lennox Gardens when a man appeared — out of the blue as it were — and grabbed hold of your wife's handbag.
Howard Where was my wife?
Mark She was on her own, walking towards Pont Street. There was a struggle and Mrs Mansfield collapsed. By the time I reached her, the man had disappeared and your wife, to say the least, was very upset. So much so — I insisted on taking her back to my car. Later, when she was feeling a little better, she asked me to call her a cab. She was still very shaken, very unsure of herself, so I took it on myself to drive her home.
Howard Did you report the incident?
Mark Yes, I did. I telephoned the police from the car and gave them a description of the man.

Howard hesitates

Howard Mr Adler, I hope you'll forgive me if I ask you one or two questions.

Mark (*faintly surprised*) Go ahead.
Howard What did the man look like who attacked my wife?
Mark He was about my height, I suppose. He was wearing jeans and what appeared to be a red blazer.
Howard Would you recognize him, if you saw him again?
Mark I doubt it. Although, curiously enough, at the time I had the feeling that I'd seen him before somewhere. I've been trying to place him. In fact, it's been bugging me, I usually remember people. (*Shaking his head*) I must be mistaken.

A brief pause

Howard (*thoughtfully*) The man got hold of my wife, grabbed her handbag, and there was a struggle?
Mark Yes.
Howard And that's all?
Mark (*puzzled*) That's all?
Howard There wasn't a conversation? Nothing was said?
Mark Not so far as I could see. (*Pause. On reflection*) No — wait a minute! The young man did say something. He must have done because I saw your wife shake her head.
Howard (*interested in this observation*) And it was after that, after he'd spoken to her, that the struggle took place?
Mark Yes. (*A moment*) Obviously, the man demanded the handbag and your wife refused to give it to him.
Howard Did my wife tell you that?
Mark No. But I'm sure that's what happened.

Pause

(*He gazes at Howard*) What's on your mind, Mr Mansfield?

Howard hesitates

Howard Did you, at any time, get the impression that Joanna — my wife — knew the man? That they'd met before?
Mark No, I didn't. I certainly didn't. (*He becomes anxious to leave*) Now, if you'll excuse me. My car isn't on a meter and I've no wish to be clamped.
Howard Of course! Forgive me! I'm sorry to have kept you.

Howard and Mark exit

Act I, Scene 1   11

A moment later, Howard returns and, quickly crosses to the desk. He opens the cupboard and takes out the handbag. He stands holding the bag and looking towards the conservatory. It is obvious that he cannot make up his mind whether to confront Joanna with the handbag or leave the situation until later

A noise is heard from the conservatory. Howard puts the bag down on the desk

Joanna enters and crosses to the drinks cabinet

Howard hesitates, then moves in front of the desk, deliberately concealing the handbag from Joanna's view. Joanna starts searching for a particular bottle

Slight pause

Joanna There doesn't seem to be any brandy.
Howard I believe there's some in the dining-room. (*Hesitantly*) Shall I fetch it?
Joanna No. Don't bother. I'll have a Scotch.
Howard Before I forget. Your mother telephoned. She's had another fall, I'm afraid.
Joanna Oh, God! Not another one? That's the third this month.
Howard Yes, I know.
Joanna Is it serious?
Howard I don't think so, but it's difficult to tell with your mother.

Howard watches as Joanna pours herself a large whisky and adds a little soda

Pause

Are you feeling any better?
Joanna I'm much better than I was. I thought I'd never stop shaking. I don't know what I'd have done if Mr Adler hadn't appeared on the scene. (*She tastes her drink; it is obviously to her liking*) I gather he's an art dealer?
Howard Yes. He has a gallery in St James's. A very nice gallery. It was broken into about six months ago. You must have read about it?

Joanna gives a vague nod and turns away from the cabinet, intent on returning to the conservatory with her drink

Don't go, Joanna! I want to talk to you.

Joanna I'm sorry, Howard. I don't feel like talking.
Howard It's important.
Joanna I really don't wish to talk. Not now. I had a nasty experience this afternoon and I'm trying hard to forget it.
Howard I can understand that. Well understand it. And I'd like to help you.
Joanna There's nothing you can do, Howard.
Howard (*quietly*) I think perhaps there is.

Joanna looks at Howard, struck by the tone of voice

To start with I can return your handbag. (*He turns, reveals the bag, and picks it up*)
Joanna (*completely taken aback*) How did that get here?
Howard (*moving down to Joanna*) Someone delivered it ...
Joanna Delivered it?
Howard Yes.
Joanna (*tersely; putting down her drink*) Who?
Howard (*his eyes on her*) I don't know. Grace came to see me. When she left, your bag was outside the front door.
Joanna Why on earth would someone take the trouble to steal my bag and then return it?
Howard (*opening the bag*) I can't imagine why. I was hoping you'd be able to answer that question. Anyway, you've been lucky. You don't appear to have lost anything.

Joanna stares at him, a worried expression on her face

Your keys are here. Your credit cards are intact. There's money in your wallet ... Oh! And you've still got this interesting little toy. (*He produces the alarm*)

Pause

How long have you had this?

No response

How long have you been carrying this around with you?
Joanna (*tremulously*) I don't know. I can't remember ... I just don't know ...
Howard Where did you get it from?

No response

Who gave it to you?

Act I, Scene 1   13

Joanna No-one gave it to me. I bought it. (*Tensely*) Howard, please! I'm not feeling well. I really don't want to talk, not at the moment ...
Howard I'm sorry, Joanna. But I do! Why do you need an alarm like this? Who is it you're frightened of? Is it the man who stole your handbag?
Joanna (*convincingly dismissing the suggestion*) No! No, I'd never set eyes on him before.
Howard Then who is it?
Joanna (*evasively; not looking at him*) I'm not frightened of anyone. It's just that the papers are full of such terrible things these days — women being raped; people being mugged, especially in London. I—I thought if I carried an alarm of some sort I'd feel safer ...
Howard Joanna, during the past three weeks or so you've been a different person. You've looked worried and distracted the whole time. Now please tell me: who is it, or what is it, you're worried about? I've got to know!
Joanna I'm not worried about anything. You're just imagining things.
Howard Did I imagine seeing you in a taxi the night I went to the theatre? The night you said you'd taken a sleeping pill and gone to bed early?

Silence

Well, Joanna?

No response

Well?

Still no response

If you ask me, you're the one with the imagination. That story about the dog was convincing, utterly convincing, I believed every word of it, until you couldn't remember what you'd told me. (*After an appreciable pause*) What happened that afternoon? What really happened?
Joanna I told you what happened.

Howard stares at her for a moment, then produces the bank statement

Howard This is your last bank statement ... The one you received two weeks ago. (*He reads*) A thousand pounds — cash. Ten days later, you transferred fifteen thousand pounds from your deposit account into your current account and immediately cashed a cheque for fifteen thousand. Why?

Silence

Why did you suddenly need fifteen thousand pounds in cash?

Still no response

    Joanna, please! (*Controlling his anger*) Sooner or later, you've got to confide in me ...
Joanna (*after a tense moment; hesitating*) I'd like to confide in you, Howard.
Howard Then why don't you?
Joanna Because we'd be bound to fall out, and quite frankly, I just couldn't face up to a row at the moment.
Howard (*kindly; not in any way reproachful*) Whatever you say to me, whatever you tell me, there won't be a row. I shall simply listen to what you've got to say and do my best to help you.

Pause

Joanna is obviously moved by this statement

Joanna Do you mean that?
Howard Yes, I do. You need help. Quite apart from Grace, other people have noticed the change that's come over you. You can't go on keeping this problem to yourself. If you do you'll be ill.

Joanna turns back to the cabinet and picks up her drink. Pause. It would appear that she is trying to decide whether to confide in Howard

    Please, Joanna! Let's talk!

A long pause

Joanna You've got this dinner tonight. We'll talk when you get back.
Howard Let's talk now, Joanna.
Joanna No, later. (*She sees Howard's expression*) Please, Howard! I'm terribly tired and there are still moments when I just can't stop shaking.

Pause

Howard Very well. We'll do as you suggest. But that's a promise?
Joanna Yes, it is.

Howard gazes at her for a moment

    We'll talk later. That really is a promise, Howard.

Act I, Scene 1   15

Howard All right, my dear. (*He puts the bank statement down and turns away from Joanna*)

The telephone rings

Joanna starts to replenish her drink from the bottle of Scotch. Howard answers the telephone

(*Into the phone*) Hallo? ...(*He pauses, frowning*) Yes, you've got the right number. Who is it you want? ...

Joanna turns and looks at him

(*Into the phone*) Oh! Just a minute. (*To Joanna*) It's for you ...
Joanna (*not moving*) Who is it?
Howard It's a Mrs Clayton.

Pause

Howard offers Joanna the phone, but to his surprise she stands completely still, almost frozen

Don't you want to take it?

Joanna finally shakes her head. Howard looks at the telephone, not quite sure what to do

Joanna (*suddenly*) Put the phone down!

Howard is taken aback by the unmistakable note of desperation in her voice

Please, Howard! (*Almost beseeching him*) Please do as I ask! We'll talk later, I promise you. I promise you, Howard!

Joanna drops the glass she is holding and rushes out of the room

The Lights fade

Scene 2

The same. Later that day

Joanna enters from the conservatory. She is wearing the same dress and is finishing painting her fingernails. She looks both agitated and worried as she puts the tiny bottle of red nail enamel on the desk and hurries out into the hall

After a moment front door is heard opening

Perry (*off*) Hi!
Joanna (*off*) You're late, Perry.
Perry (*off*) Couldn't agree more. Horrendous traffic. Been sitting in the Merc. for hours …

Perry Kingsley enters, followed by Joanna. Perry is wearing a summer-style anorak. He turns and looks at Joanna

(*Impatiently*) Now, what's this all about? Why send for me? I have an important meeting and I'm late already.
Joanna You know perfectly well why I've sent for you! That woman telephoned …
Perry That woman?
Joanna Mrs Clayton!
Perry (*apparently surprised*) Mrs Clayton telephoned here?
Joanna Yes.
Perry When? When was this?
Joanna This afternoon. About five o'clock.
Perry What happened? Did you talk to her?
Joanna No. Howard answered the phone and I refused to take the call.
Perry (*urgently*) Well — what happened? What did you say? What did you tell Howard?
Joanna (*quietly; her eyes on him*) I didn't tell him anything.
Perry But you must have said something! Didn't he question you? Didn't he want to know who she was? (*Pause*) Well?

Joanna glares at him

Why are you looking at me like that? (*He moves closer to her*) You surely don't think I was responsible for that phone call?
Joanna Weren't you?
Perry Of course I wasn't!
Joanna I don't believe you. You told her to phone me. I know you did! You're trying to frighten me.

Act I, Scene 2   17

Perry Frighten you? Why in God's name would I want to frighten you?
Joanna Because I've refused to pay you any more money, that's why! I gave you the fifteen thousand on the strict understanding that I wouldn't hear from that woman and that this business would be settled, once and for all. And it isn't settled!
Perry Wait a minute! Let's get this straight! *You didn't give me anything!* Every penny of that money — every cent — went to that wretched woman. If I've told you once, I've told you a hundred times; I haven't made a buck out of this business. Not only that. It's been a source of worry to me! A constant source of worry, if you must know!
Joanna Then I've got some news for you, Perry. Your worries are over. At long last, thank goodness, I've come to my senses.
Perry And what's that supposed to mean?
Joanna It means I'm about to do something I should have done ages ago. I'm going to confide in Howard. I'm going to tell him the whole story.
Perry (*with alarm*) But you can't do that! You mustn't do it! If Howard takes it into his head to consult someone we're in trouble! Both of us! Deep trouble!
Joanna I'm in trouble as it is, and I simply can't go on like this. I'm worried to death. I can't sleep at night and I'm drinking too much. Far too much ...

Perry is angry and not a little scared

Perry And when do you propose having this interesting conversation with your husband?
Joanna Tonight. As soon as Howard gets back from a dinner at the Grosvenor House.
Perry And what happens if Howard decides to talk to someone? A lawyer? The police maybe?
Joanna (*fatalistically*) So be it ...
Perry So be it, be damned! If you think I'm going to let Howard take over after all the trouble I've taken ...
Joanna (*stopping him*) It's no use, Perry! I've made my mind up and nothing you can do, or say, will make me change it.
Perry (*losing control of his feelings; an unmistakable threat*) Now you listen to me, Joanna!
Joanna I have listened to you, and look what's happened! The fact is, I should never have listened to you in the first place.
Perry Well, you did! And you're going to listen to me again! (*He grabs hold of Joanna*)

Joanna looks astonished

You're not talking to Howard tonight, or any other night! You're not going to tell him about Mrs Clayton, about me, about the bungalow, about anything! You understand?
Joanna (*distinctly shaken, struggling to release herself*) Have you taken leave of your senses!
Perry I'm warning you! If you talk to Howard ...
Joanna Let go of me! (*She struggles*) Do you hear what I say?
Perry If you talk to Howard about this business, if you consult anyone other than me, you'll live to regret it.
Joanna Will you please leave go of me! (*Struggling*) Leave go, Perry!

A tense pause — then Perry slowly releases Joanna. Joanna, both angry and greatly shaken, backs away from him

I think you'd better go!
Perry (*still threatening*) You heard what I said?
Joanna Yes, I heard. (*She moves further away from him*) Now, please go!
Perry I'm not leaving here until you promise me ——
Joanna I'm promising you nothing! You must be out of your mind to behave this way!

Perry hesitates, then seeing the state that Joanna is in, and realizing the mistake he has made, he makes a light-hearted attempt to pacify her

Perry I'm sorry, Joanna. I don't know what got into me. I didn't mean to hurt you. I apologize ...
Joanna (*quietly; yet still angered*) Please go, Perry.
Perry I understand your position, Joanna. Believe me, I do. You've got a problem with Howard. I realize that. But all I'm asking you to do ——
Joanna All I'm asking you to do — *is go*! Now, please do that ——
Perry Be reasonable, darling. I've apologized. What else can I do?
Joanna I want you to go, Perry!

As Joanna reaches the desk she notices the large stiletto type letter opener and quickly picks it up. She faces him with the letter opener

Perry freezes

Do as I say! Leave me ...

An appreciable pause, then Perry makes a desperate attempt to save the situation

Act I, Scene 2   19

Perry Now don't be a fool. You're not going to use that thing. You know damn well you're not. (*Smiling*) You look ridiculous. Put it down, Joanna — and let's talk.

Joanna stands firm, shaking her head, determined that he should leave

Joanna From now on, the only person I'm talking to is Howard.

This is too much for Perry who, once again, fails to control his anger

Perry Then you've asked for it! You stupid bitch! (*He produces a gun, a squat .44 magnum, from the pocket of his coat*) Now put that thing down!

There is a stunned silence, then a terrified Joanna slowly puts the letter opener back on the desk

Perry crosses to her, with the intention of picking the letter opener up. In doing so he momentarily takes his eyes off Joanna. Joanna, hardly aware of what she is doing, grabs hold of his arm in an attempt to get possession of the gun

The brief struggle immediately becomes heated, almost vicious. It is brought to a climax by the accidental firing of the gun

Perry staggers backwards, clutching his body and finally collapsing

Joanna Perry! (*With alarm*) Oh, my God! (*She drops the gun she is holding and goes to Perry's assistance. In tears, she kneels beside Perry*)

Perry is obviously in pain and on the verge of losing consciousness. After a moment, realizing that help is urgently needed, Joanna rises and rushes to the phone. She is beside herself as she starts dialing

The number is ringing out at the other end when there is a noise of the front door closing. Joanna, taken by surprise, slams the phone down and turns towards the hall

Howard enters. He is wearing a dinner jacket and a scarf is draped across his shoulders

(*Rushing towards him*) Howard! Thank God, you've come back! There's been an accident! A dreadful accident!

Howard takes hold of Joanna, but his eyes are on Perry

Howard It's Perry Kingsley.
Joanna Yes ...
Howard What happened? What's he doing here?
Joanna Perry had a gun. He threatened me with it, I tried to ... (*Beside herself*) Howard, I'm frightened and desperately worried. Please help me!
Howard Have you sent for anyone?
Joanna No. I—I was just about to ...
Howard Fetch a rug while I ring for an ambulance.

Joanna quickly exits

Howard takes a brief look at Perry, then crosses to the phone. He dials

Pause

Howard (*into phone*) ... I'm speaking from twenty-eight Clifton Place, Holland Park. There's been an accident and we need an ambulance straight away! ... That's right, twenty-eight Clifton Place, it's off Ladbroke Square. (*He looks across at Perry*) Please hurry! It's urgent! Very urgent. (*He replaces the receiver. He collects a cushion from the sofa and takes it down to Perry. He places the cushion under Perry's head*)

Joanna returns with a rug

Howard takes the rug from Joanna and covers Perry's body with it. As he rises he suddenly sees the gun on the floor

That's Perry's gun?
Joanna Yes, I swear I didn't shoot him, Howard. He threatened me, there was a struggle and the gun went off.
Howard What was Perry doing here?
Joanna I—I sent for him. (*She bursts into tears; desperately*) Please help me — tell me what I should do ... (*Frightened*) Oughtn't we to send for the police?

There is a tense pause. Howard suddenly reaches a decision

Howard Now, listen! And listen carefully! I want you to go down to the cottage ...
Joanna (*with surprise*) The cottage?
Howard Yes.
Joanna (*puzzled*) When?
Howard Now! Immediately!

Act I, Scene 2

Joanna But why the cottage? I don't see what good my going down there will do.

Howard (*with authority*) If you want me to help you, then you must do exactly as I tell you. Now, listen! Go to the end of the road and pick up a taxi. (*He looks at his watch*) There's a train for Sutton Valence at eight twenty. I've caught it many times and you should catch it tonight. If you don't there's another one at nine something. Whatever you do, don't talk to anyone on the train. When you get to Sutton Valence — no matter how tired you feel — don't take a cab. Walk to the cottage. Is that clear? Absolutely clear?

Joanna Yes ...

Howard And whatever happens, don't leave the cottage. Not until I tell you to. I'll phone you as soon as I can.

Howard quickly leads Joanna into the hall

There is a pause

Howard returns carrying a pair of gloves. His manner is tense and urgent. His thoughts are on a deliberate plan of action. He places the gloves on the arm of the sofa; he removes the scarf, crosses the room and picks up the gun. Slowly making use of the scarf, he wipes the gun completely free of fingerprints. He then kneels down by the body, puts the gun into Perry's hand and once again establishes Perry's finger-prints on the weapon. Once this is done, Howard carefully registers his own prints on the gun, finally placing it near the body

There are now only two sets of fingerprints on the gun, Perry's and Howard's

Howard takes off his jacket, rips open his collar and bow-tie, and deliberately spoils the look of his jacket. He puts on his jacket, crosses to the sofa and picks up the pair of gloves. He quietly surveys the room as he puts on the gloves. Then he quickly goes to work in an attempt to convey the impression that the room has been thoroughly searched and that a desperate struggle has recently taken place. He turns over chairs, upsets table lamps, scatters various objects onto the floor, and deliberately ransacks the drawers of his desk. Finally, after taking stock of his efforts, he picks up the phone and dials

Pause

(*Into the phone; tense and urgent*) Police? ... My name is Mansfield — Howard Mansfield. ... I'm speaking from my home in Holland Park.

Black-out

Scene 3

The same. Three hours later

The room is virtually back to normal and Perry Kingsley has been taken to hospital

Howard enters from the hall with the Chief Inspector — Chris Coldwell. Howard wears casual clothes. Chris is a shrewd-looking man in his early forties

Chris I'm sorry to disturb you, Mr Mansfield.
Howard (*pleasantly; yet a shade surprised*) That's all right.

Chris surveys the room

Chris I can see you haven't wasted any time. You appear to be pretty straight.
Howard What can I do for you, Inspector?
Chris Well — first of all, I thought you might like to know that Mr Kingsley's in intensive care and likely to remain there for some time.
Howard Yes, I know. I telephoned the hospital. How is he? I couldn't get any information out of them.
Chris If you ask me, he's lucky to be alive. Let's hope he stays that way.
Howard Is he conscious?
Chris Yes, he's conscious.
Howard And able to talk?
Chris Just about. But he's no help to us, I'm afraid. Or you too, for that matter.
Howard What does that mean?
Chris It means that — for some reason best known to himself — Mr Kingsley refuses to make a statement. (*Pause*) Mr Mansfield, shortly after you and your solicitor left the station, I received a call from a colleague of mine in Chelsea. If he's got his facts right, and I'm sure he has — it would appear that your wife had a very nasty experience this afternoon.
Howard Yes, she did. (*Puzzled*) She was on her way back from the hairdresser's when a young man attacked her.
Chris In Lennox Gardens?
Howard That's right.
Chris Why didn't you tell me about this, sir?
Howard I didn't think it was important since it had nothing to do with Perry Kingsley and the events of this evening.
Chris What happened exactly?
Howard My wife's handbag was stolen.

Act I, Scene 3   23

Chris Was Mrs Mansfield hurt at all?
Howard No. But obviously she was shaken. Fortunately a stranger — a Mr Adler — came to her rescue and brought her home. (*A moment; he stares at Chris*) But why are you interested in my wife?
Chris It's just that in the light of this information about Mrs Mansfield, I'm somewhat puzzled. (*A tiny pause*) As I understand it, the incident in Lennox Gardens occurred at about half-past four. So it must have been about — well, let's say — five fifteen when Mrs Mansfield arrived home.

Howard hesitates, then gives a little nod

An hour or so later, according to your statement — your wife suddenly took it into her head to go down to your cottage near Sutton Valence.
Howard That's correct.
Chris Wasn't that a little odd, sir?
Howard Odd?
Chris Your wife couldn't have been feeling well. She'd just recently had a very nasty experience.
Howard She wasn't feeling at all well. She was quite shaken in fact. But you don't know my wife, Inspector.
Chris Meaning what, sir?
Howard Meaning — my wife never gets her priorities right when it comes to taking care of herself. I've known her play tennis with a swollen ankle and go skiing with a temperature of a hundred and three. It's a problem I've had to live with.
Chris I see, sir.
Howard Are you married, Inspector?
Chris No, sir. I'm not married.
Howard Then I doubt very much whether you do see.

Chris smiles

Chris Tell me again what happened after your wife left for Sutton Valence.
Howard I made myself a cup of coffee, took several telephone calls and got ready for a dinner at the Grosvenor House. On my way to the hotel I suddenly realized that I'd left my wallet, credit cards, and wrist-watch on a table in the bedroom.
Chris So you turned the car round and came back?
Howard Yes.
Chris Go on, sir.
Howard Is it necessary for me to repeat what I've already told you?
Chris No, sir. Not if you don't wish to. But it might be helpful. You may recall something which you quite inadvertently overlooked.

Howard hesitates

Howard As soon as I entered the room I saw Perry — Mr Kingsley. I was staggered. Bewildered, in fact. The room was in a turmoil and there were papers all over the place.
Chris What was he doing at that precise moment?
Howard He was searching the desk, obviously looking for something ...
Chris Go on, sir.
Howard I said, "Perry, what the hell are you doing here? What's going on?" He swung round and it was then that I realized he had a gun ...
Chris The gun was in his hand?
Howard Yes, it was.
Chris And then what happened?
Howard Rather stupidly, I suppose, I approached him. At that moment the phone rang and, without thinking, he turned and looked at it. I immediately threw myself at him. There was a struggle and somehow or other — God knows how it happened — the gun went off.

Pause

Chris Have you any idea how Mr Kingsley got into the house?
Howard No, I haven't. There's no break-in as such. He must have had a key.
Chris We didn't find one on him, sir. (*Pause*) You say, when you entered the room he appeared to be searching for something?
Howard Yes.
Chris Have you any idea what it was?

A moment

Howard It could only have been money. I can't think of anything else.
Chris How well did you and your wife know Mr Kingsley?
Howard When he was married to Grace, a friend of my wife's, we used to see quite a lot of him. However, after the divorce he uprooted himself and went to live in Ibiza.
Chris We've been trying to get hold of Mrs Kingsley, but without success. There's no response from the number you gave us.
Howard Yes. I'm sorry. I forgot. She's in Hertfordshire. I don't know where exactly. She'll be back some time tomorrow.

Brief pause

Chris Does your wife know about Mr Kingsley, sir?
Howard Yes, she does. I telephoned the cottage immediately after you interviewed me.

Act I, Scene 3   25

Chris What was her reaction?
Howard She was stunned, of course, and terribly upset.
Chris Did she venture an opinion as to what Mr Kingsley was doing here?
Howard No, she didn't. Like me, she was completely bewildered.

A moment

How the devil did Perry get hold of a gun? I thought that was impossible these days.
Chris Nothing's impossible if you have the right contacts.

Howard nods and is about to comment when the telephone rings

Howard (*looking towards the desk*) Excuse me. (*He crosses to the telephone. Into the phone*) ... Yes, speaking. ... I beg your pardon? Oh! Just a moment ... (*To Chris*) This is for you, Inspector.

Chris joins Howard and takes the phone from him

Chris Thank you, sir.

Howard turns away from the desk and moves down to the drinks cabinet

Whilst Chris is on the phone Howard deliberately busies himself at the cabinet, putting glasses away, rearranging bottles, etc. He would appear to be uninterested in the Inspector's conversation

(*Into the phone*) ... Chief Inspector Coldwell. ... (*None too happy*) All right, I'll hold ...(*As he is kept waiting impatiently, he takes stock of the various articles on the desk, including the tiny bottle of nail lacquer. He picks up the bottle, casually looks at it, then hearing a voice on the phone, immediately puts it down. Into the phone; irritated*) Yes, I'm Chief Inspector Coldwell. I've already said so! ... Well — *put him on*! (*A moment*) What is this Sergeant? How many girls have you got working for you these days? ... Bully for you! Now, what's the problem? ... (*A long pause; obviously alerted to something*) How did you come by this information? (*Pause; quietly*) I see. ... When was this? ... (*Pause*) Go on, Sergeant. What else did he tell you? ... (*Long pause*) Yes, that is interesting. Very! ... (*An appreciable pause*) No, don't do that! I'd like to talk to him myself. Get one of your many underlings to give him a cup of tea. I'll come straight back. (*He replaces the receiver*)

Howard turns

Chris (*after a moment's consideration*) Mr Mansfield, do you, by any chance, know a young man called Winter — Rex Winter?
Howard (*shaking his head*) No. Who is he?
Chris He's the man who stole your wife's handbag. A patrol car picked him up about an hour ago. He's made a statement in which he claims to have returned the bag and its contents. He says he brought it here, this afternoon. Is that true?
Howard Yes, I suppose it is. He left the bag — or someone did — outside the front door.
Chris Outside the front door?
Howard Yes. Mrs Kingsley found it when she was leaving here.
Chris (*after a thoughtful pause*) I see. Thank you, sir. Now, if you'll excuse me. (*He turns, then stops*) Oh! Before I go. I wonder if you would satisfy my curiosity? (*He returns to the desk and picks up the tiny bottle*) Is this yours?

Howard hardly hears the question, he is lost in thought

Howard What did you say?
Chris Is this yours, sir?
Howard What is it?
Chris It's a bottle of nail lacquer. (*He looks at the label*) Magic Fingers …
Howard Of course, it isn't mine! It's my wife's …
Chris (*smiling*) Yes, of course! Stupid of me! (*He returns the bottle to the desk*) That's all I wanted to know, sir. (*He moves towards the hall*) We shall be in touch, Mr Mansfield.

Chris exits

Howard stares after him, obviously puzzled, then he crosses to the desk and picks up the bottle of nail lacquer. He looks at the bottle

The Lights fade

Scene 4

The same. The next morning.

It is a bright day and the window looking on to the garden is partly open

Grace is sitting on the sofa listening to Howard, who is standing near her. It is fairly obvious that, at some point, Grace has been upset

Howard That's it, Grace. There's nothing else I can tell you. I just hope the police believe me and accept the fact that the shooting was an accident.
Grace What does your lawyer think?

Act I, Scene 4   27

Howard He keeps saying he doesn't think I've anything to worry about, but — I am worried, of course. Who wouldn't be?
Grace Have the newspapers been on to you?
Howard Not only me. They've even questioned Hilary. I've just put the phone down on her.
Grace It was such a shock, Howard — suddenly hearing your name on the radio. For a moment, I was stunned! I just couldn't believe it. The funny thing is, I hardly ever listen to the radio when I'm driving. I can't remember the last time I switched it on. (*There is a pause, then she rises*) What does the hospital say? I take it you've spoken to them?
Howard I was on to them first thing this morning. The news isn't good, I'm afraid.
Grace With all his faults, I'm very fond of Perry. After the divorce I tried to hate him, I really did. I kept telling myself he was no good, no good to anyone, and that I really must put him out of my mind once and for all. But he only had to pick up the phone, I only had to hear his voice again ...
Howard I know ...

Pause

Grace finally manages to control her feelings

Grace Howard, you've put me in the picture as to what happened between you and Perry, but you haven't told me what he was doing here? Why he came to the house?
Howard (*avoiding looking at her*) I don't know why he came here, Grace. And not only that, I don't know how the devil he managed to get into the house in the first place.
Grace He must have had a key.
Howard The police didn't find one on him.
Grace Then someone must have let him in.
Howard There was no-one here. The house was empty. Joanna was at the cottage and I was on my way to that wretched dinner.
Grace (*puzzled*) Yes, but — (*She hesitates*) You say Joanna was badly shaken by what happened in Lennox Gardens?
Howard Very badly shaken. (*After an uneasy pause*) Why? What's worrying you, Grace?
Grace It's just that, I find it strange that within hours of being mugged, Joanna suddenly took it into her head to go down to Sutton Valence. (*Gazing at him*) And, to be honest, Howard, I find it even more strange that you allowed her to do that.
Howard I had no choice. Joanna was determined to go to the cottage and there was simply nothing I could do about it. Good heavens, Grace, you know Joanna! Once she decides to do something, that's it!

Grace Yes, but why the cottage?
Howard She said she could rest better down there.
Grace But she'd taken a dislike to the place. She even wanted you to sell it. You told me that yourself. And there's another thing. If you couldn't stop her going to the cottage, why didn't you drive her down there, instead of letting her go by train?
Howard I—I had this dinner at the Grosvenor House. I just couldn't get out of it. (*Painfully aware that his excuse doesn't ring true, he quickly changes the subject*) Grace, there's something I want to ask you. Does the name Clayton mean anything to you? Mrs Clayton?
Grace Mrs Clayton? (*Shaking her head*) No, who is she?
Howard I don't know who she is. All I know is, she telephoned yesterday and asked for Joanna. Joanna refused to take the call. Not only that — at the mention of the woman's name she became, well — almost frightened.
Grace (*with curiousity*) What did this woman sound like?
Howard She sounded quite young, although it's difficult to tell on the phone.

The doorbell rings

Grace (*shaking her head*) I'm sorry. I've never heard of her.

The doorbell continues ringing and Howard looks towards the hall

Are you expecting anyone?
Howard No.

Howard goes out into the hall

Pause

There is the sound of voices

Chris (*off, pleasantly*) I thought I'd catch you before you left for the office, sir.
Howard (*off*) I'm glad you've called, Inspector. Mrs Kingsley's here.

Howard returns with Chris. Chris carries a valise

Howard Grace, this is Chief Inspector Coldwell.
Chris Good-morning, Mrs Kingsley. We've been trying to get in touch with you.
Grace I've been staying with some friends in Hertfordshire. I only got back this morning.

Act I, Scene 4

Chris puts his valise down by the side of one of the chairs

Chris We left a message on your answering machine, asking you to call us.
Grace I'm sorry, but I haven't been home. I heard about Perry — my ex-husband — on the car radio and came straight here.
Chris I see. (*He glances at Howard*) I imagine Mr Mansfield has already told you his version of what happened last night?

Howard registers a faint surprise at the "his version"

Grace Yes, he has.
Chris Then perhaps you'd be good enough to answer one or two questions, Mrs Kingsley? I shan't keep you long.
Grace If I can help you I will. What is it you want to ask me?
Chris Were you on friendly terms with your ex-husband?
Grace Yes, I was. Although I haven't seen a great deal of him during the past couple of years. Almost immediately after the divorce he went to live in Ibiza.
Chris Did you visit him, whilst he was in Ibiza?
Grace No, I didn't.
Chris When was the last time you saw Mr Kingsley?
Grace (*with hesitation*) We had a drink together, the day before yesterday.
Chris Was that the first time you'd seen him since his return to the UK?
Grace (*still a slight hesitation*) No. I've seen him several times.

Howard looks at her

Chris How did he strike you? Was he depressed? Worried, perhaps, about financial matters?
Grace On the contrary, he didn't seem to have a care in the world.
Chris Did Mr Kingsley mention Mrs Mansfield at all, during the course of your conversations?
Grace I can't remember. He may have done, briefly ...
Chris Do you happen to know whether he'd seen her recently? Since leaving Ibiza, that is?
Grace (*surprised by the question*) I've no reason to think so.
Chris Was Mrs Mansfield here yesterday afternoon when you called?
Grace No. She hadn't returned from the hairdresser's.
Howard (*slightly on edge*) Mrs Kingsley came to see me, Inspector. Quite apart from being a close friend of my wife's, we're business associates.
Chris Oh! Is that so, sir?
Howard And why the sudden interest in my wife?
Chris That's a good question, Mr Mansfield.

Howard Then I suggest you answer it.
Chris I will, sir. In due course. (*To Grace*) Mrs Kingsley, have you any idea why your ex-husband came here last night?
Grace No, I'm sorry. I haven't.
Chris Mr Mansfield seems to think that he was searching for something.
Grace If he was, I can't imagine what it could have been.

Chris looks at Grace for a moment

Chris Neither can I, Mrs Kingsley. (*Dismissing her*) Thank you. I won't detain you any longer.

Grace, a shade puzzled by Chris's sudden dismissal of her, crosses towards the hall, glancing at Howard as she does so

Howard realizes she is inviting him to see her out

   They both exit

Chris smiles to himself, moves down to the window and stares out

Pause

   Howard returns

I'm just admiring your garden. It's in fine shape, I must say. The flowers are magnificent.
Howard Thank you. That's my wife's department. She's the gardener.

Chris turns and joins Howard

Chris Well, sir — you'll be interested to learn we've solved one problem since we last met.
Howard Oh?
Chris (*pleasantly*) We now know how Mr Kingsley got into the house. Mrs Mansfield was expecting him and she let him in. It was as simple as that, I'm afraid.
Howard (*taken by surprise*) But that's nonsense! How the devil could she let him in? She wasn't here! She left the house before I did. If you take the trouble to read my statement you'll see that my wife left for Sutton Valence at about six o'clock, long before I came across Perry Kingsley.
Chris I have read your statement, sir. Several times. And it's occurred to me, in the light of recent developments, that you may wish to change it.

Act I, Scene 4   31

A brief, awkward silence

No? Well, maybe you'll have second thoughts when I tell you about the conversation I've had with Rex Winter. The young man who stole your wife's handbag.
Howard Right now, I'm not interested in Mr Winter or the handbag! My only concern at the moment ——
Chris (*forcefully; interrupting him*) You may not be interested in him, sir — but we are! And I'll tell you why! Rex Winter worked for Perry Kingsley in Ibiza. Not only that, he was working with him when your wife telephoned Kingsley asking him to call here.

There is an uneasy silence

Did you know about that phone call, sir? (*Pause*) Well — did you?

Howard remains silent

(*Quietly*) Mr Mansfield. I have a theory. Quite an interesting one. (*After a brief pause*) It's my opinion, when you left the house last night your wife was still here. At that point there had been no suggestion of her going down to Sutton Valence. On the way to the hotel you suddenly changed your mind about the dinner and returned home. When you arrived here you discovered that your wife had had a row with Perry Kingsley during the course of which there was a struggle and Mr Kingsley was shot.
Howard Go on …
Chris Realizing the situation your wife was in, you made up your mind to divert attention from her. "To carry the can" in fact. In other words, your statement was nothing more than a red herring. A deliberate attempt to pull the wool over our eyes.
Howard (*half humorously*) Do you believe that? Do you really believe that's what happened?
Chris Yes, sir. I do.

Howard starts laughing

Why are you laughing?
Howard Inspector, you've got a fantastic imagination. It's a great pity you don't put it to better use.
Chris What would you suggest, sir?
Howard I would suggest you write a novel. Every little actress seems to be doing it these days. So why not you? My firm would buy an option on it straightaway.

Chris Would they, sir? Well — that's nice to know. (*A moment*) One thing's for sure. If I do write a book I shall certainly know what to call it.
Howard Oh? And what's that?
Chris Magic fingers.

Pause

Howard (*puzzled*) Magic fingers?
Chris Yes, sir. (*Pause*) Mr Kingsley's clothes were sent to our Forensic Department. Their report drew my attention to certain marks — tiny red spots — on Mr Kingsley's jacket. I was puzzled. I couldn't account for them. (*He turns, picks up his valise, and moves towards the hall*) That is — not until I noticed the nail polish your wife uses.

Chris exits

The Lights quickly fade

Scene 5

The same. Early evening that day

Howard enters from the hall carrying some books. Having attended a somewhat acrimonious Board meeting, he looks tired and on edge as he crosses to the desk, puts down the books and picks up the phone. He hesitates for a second or two, then quickly dials

There is a pause, whilst Howard listens impatiently

Howard (*into the phone; unable to control his irritation*) Grace, this is the second message I've left on your machine! What happened this afternoon? Why weren't you at the Board meeting? We waited almost an hour for you! Please phone me the moment you get in ...(*He slams down the phone and somewhat depressed, turns away from the desk. As he does so he glances into the garden and looks surprised as if he sees someone approaching the house. He slides open the window; calling*) What is it you want?

Brief pause

Rex Winter comes into view. He is in his thirties and wears a red blazer

Rex Mr Mansfield?
Howard Yes.

Act I, Scene 5

Rex Could I possibly have a word with your wife, sir?
Howard My wife isn't here at the moment. What is it you want? Who are you?
Rex My name is Winter. Rex Winter.
Howard (*with surprise*) Winter? (*Glaring at him*) You're the man that attacked my wife in Lennox Gardens.
Rex Yes — and I'd very much like to apologize to her and explain what happened.
Howard (*intensely angry; attempting to grab hold of him*) You would, would you?
Rex (*retreating*) Mr Mansfield, I know how you feel! I know only too well how you feel! But please listen to me!

Howard stares at Rex for a moment, then indicates that he can enter

Howard All right! Say what you've got to say and be quick about it!

Rex comes into the room

Rex I'm sorry about yesterday. I had no wish to hurt Mrs Mansfield. Believe me, that was not my intention.
Howard You could have fooled my wife.
Rex (*contrite*) How is Mrs Mansfield?
Howard She'll survive. Now, what the devil is this all about? Why steal my wife's handbag and then return it? I take it, it was you that returned the bag?
Rex Yes, it was. And please believe me, Mr Mansfield — immediately after I'd taken it I realized what a fool I'd been.
Howard Let's get this straight! Are you telling me you regretted stealing the bag and that's why you returned it?
Rex Yes.
Howard And you expect me to believe that story?
Rex It's the truth, Mr Mansfield. I was worried about your wife. I kept wondering if I'd hurt her. Besides ... (*He hesitates*)
Howard Besides, what?
Rex Stealing the bag wasn't my idea ...
Howard Then whose idea was it?
Rex Perry Kingsley's. I've been working for Perry — doing odd jobs for him. He said if I could lay my hands on your wife's handbag he'd make it worth my while. (*Shaking his head*) I shouldn't have listened to him of course. I've regretted it ever since.
Howard Why did Perry want the handbag?
Rex I can only think of one reason. Perry was curious about well-known people. People like you, Mr Mansfield. He went out of his way to gather information about them. Your wife's keys would have enabled him to search your house whenever he felt like it.

Howard is staring at Rex, not sure whether to accept this explanation or not

Howard What happened when you didn't deliver the bag? What did you tell Perry?
Rex I told him your wife put up a fight, refused to hand over the bag — and I panicked. Unfortunately, later in the day the police picked me up and I was questioned by a Chief Inspector Coldwell. In fact, he never stopped questioning me. I was with him the best part of two hours. In the end he let me go, but ... (*He looks at Howard*) ... If Mrs Mansfield brings charges against me ...
Howard You're in trouble?
Rex Yes. So — I'd be grateful, more than grateful, Mr Mansfield, if you could persuade your wife to forget what happened yesterday afternoon.

Pause

Howard My wife was upset and extremely angry. She still is.
Rex I appreciate that, and I'm sorry.

A pause during which Howard is quietly trying to make up his mind about Rex

Howard All right. I'll have a word with my wife and we'll see what she says.
Rex (*somewhat relieved*) Thank you. I won't take up any more of your time. (*He moves towards the window*)
Howard No, wait!

Rex turns

You say Inspector Coldwell questioned you for almost two hours?
Rex Yes. Once he discovered I'd worked for Perry in Ibiza he just never let up. He wanted to know how long I'd known Perry, who worked at the café, who came there, and what my job was ...
Howard What was your job, Winter?
Rex I was employed as a waiter, but most of the time I was just a dogsbody. At Perry's beck and call from ten in the morning until well after midnight. Originally, I was a photographer on the *Sunday Herald*. I went out to Ibiza on an assignment, fell in love with the place, and emigrated. (*He shakes his head*) I must have been out of my tiny mind! I'd only been there three months when my equipment was stolen and I was up to my ears in debt.
Howard And Perry came to the rescue?
Rex Yes. I kept bumping into him on the beach. He must have heard I was hard up because one morning, much to my surprise, he asked me if I'd like to work for him. (*Bitterly*) I was a fool of course, I ought never to have left England. When the café closed I tried to get my old job back, but the editor wouldn't even see me.

Act I, Scene 5

Howard Were you surprised when the café closed down and Perry returned to London?
Rex I was staggered, and so was everyone else.
Howard Did you tell the Inspector that?
Rex Yes, I did.
Howard And what did he say?
Rex He made no comment, just kept on asking questions. He even wanted to know if Perry's ex-wife — Grace Kingsley — was a friend of mine. I assured him she wasn't, but I don't think he believed me.
Howard Have you met Mrs Kingsley?
Rex No, but I've seen her. She came to the café one evening.
Howard (*staring at him*) Grace Kingsley came to the café?
Rex Yes. But she won't remember me. We were very busy that night and I was dashing all over the place.
Howard What was she doing in Ibiza?
Rex I imagine she was on holiday.
Howard Was she staying with Perry?
Rex No. She was staying in a villa on the south side of the island. It belongs to a friend of Perry's. An Englishman called Adler.
Howard Adler? Mark Adler?
Rex That's right. Mark Adler. He's an art dealer.

Howard is certainly surprised and for a brief moment appears lost in thought

(*Puzzled by his reaction*) Do you know him?

Pause

Howard (*at length*) We've met.
Rex He's got a fantastic house. There isn't another one like it on the island. Must have cost a fortune.

A moment

Howard You say Adler was a friend of Perry's?
Rex Well — yes. I wouldn't say they were close friends, but Adler used to drop in the café most mornings, if only for a chat. There was an article about him in the local rag a couple of months back. It said he had houses all over ——

Both men hear a noise in the hall

Howard crosses the room

Howard (*calling into the hall*) Who is that?
Joanna (*off: after a moment, calling back*) It's me, Howard. I'll be with you in a minute.

Pause

Rex It's your wife?
Howard Yes. (*He hesitates*) Stay here!
Rex I'd very much like to have a word with Mrs Mansfield.
Howard I'll talk to her and we'll see what she says.

Howard quickly exits

As soon as Howard exits, Rex sits on the sofa, takes a mobile phone out of his pocket and punches a number. A long pause. The number is ringing but there is obviously no reply. He replaces the phone in his pocket and sits for a while quietly taking stock of his surroundings. Eventually he rises, having decided to take a closer look at the books and pictures

Rex has completed his tour of the room and is about to return to the sofa when a sudden thought occurs to him. He takes a second look at one of the pictures — "Flowers On A Tray"

Howard returns

I've spoken to my wife and I'm afraid she doesn't wish to see you.
Rex (*disappointed*) Oh!
Howard I think she's wise. It would only upset her again. However, you can put your mind at rest. My wife wishes to forget what happened yesterday afternoon.
Rex I'm relieved to hear that! Very relieved! And thank you for your help, Mr Mansfield. (*He crosses to the window*) If I can be of assistance at any time, I'm in the book.

Rex exits

Howard watches his departure, then moves back to the hall

Howard (*raising his voice*) It's all right, Joanna. He's gone …

Pause

Joanna slowly emerges from the hall. She looks distinctly worried

Act I, Scene 5   37

For a moment they stand taking each other in

Joanna Do you believe what that young man told you?
Howard Not entirely. But then, I'd hesitate to believe anyone who worked for Perry Kingsley.
Joanna He worked for Perry?
Howard Both here and in Ibiza. And if Winter's telling the truth it was Perry that wanted your handbag. But we'll talk about that later. Right now, we've other things to talk about. Why did you leave the cottage? I told you not to. Have the police contacted you?
Joanna No. No-one's been near me. (*Desperately*) I'm sorry, Howard, I just couldn't stay at the cottage a minute longer! I lay awake the whole of last night worrying — about what might happen to you. (*Almost beside herself*) It's no use, I can't let you take the blame for what happened. I just can't.
Howard I rather think it's no longer a question of my taking the blame.

Joanna looks at him, surprised

Your nail varnish left a mark on Perry's clothing. Not only that — the police know about the phone call you made, insisting that you see Perry.

An uneasy silence

Why did you want to see him?

No reply

You promised to confide in me. Remember? Now's the time to keep that promise. (*Pause*) Was Perry blackmailing you?

There is still no reply from Joanna, and Howard, in a sudden burst of anger, grabs hold of her

Howard Joanna, answer me! Was Perry Kingsley blackmailing you?

Again silence

Was he?

The Lights quickly fade to Black-out

The Curtain *falls*

ACT II

Scene 1

The same. Immediately following

The action is virtually continuous. Howard is still holding Joanna who has obviously been in tears. Howard has calmed down somewhat and is beginning to regret his outburst

Joanna Howard, please don't be angry with me. I've had the most dreadful night.

Pause

Howard releases her

Howard I'm sorry, Joanna. Did I hurt you?
Joanna No. No. I'll be all right in a minute. (*She slowly moves away from him*)

Pause

Howard Would you like a drink?

Joanna hesitates

Joanna Yes, I would, but I'm not having one. I've been drinking far too much lately. (*She crosses to the sofa and sits*)

Pause

Howard moves nearer the sofa and stands staring down at her

There is a short silence between them, then Joanna looks up and their eyes meet

This business with Perry started a little while back whilst you were in New York. It was the night my father had his first heart attack. I had a call from

Act II, Scene 1

the doctor telling me that he'd been taken to Milton Cross hospital. My car was in the garage but I'd lost my licence and I'd been warned that, under no circumstances, must I drive.

Howard nods

On top of which it was a foul night, quite foggy in places. I did my best to get hold of a driver, but it was hopeless. Quite hopeless. (*Slight pause. She turns away from him*) In the end, I went down to the garage and got the car out ...

Pause

Howard (*softly; concerned*) Go on ...
Joanna I knew the risk I was taking, I knew it only too well! ... But I was desperately worried about my father ... (*Trying hard to control her tears*) I drove carefully, very carefully, but just before Milton Cross the fog got worse and I took the wrong turning. It must have been ten minutes before I realized that I'd lost my way and was driving down a country lane. Suddenly, to my amazement, I saw a building immediately in front of me. I slammed the brakes on, the car skidded, and crashed into a bungalow.
Howard Go on, Joanna.
Joanna I panicked, Howard. I jumped out of the car and ran into the lane. I felt that, at all cost, I must get as far away from the car as possible. Eventually, I reached a main road. There was a flashing light on the corner and I suddenly realized it was coming from a pub. I staggered in, ordered myself a Scotch, and was drinking it when I saw a man staring at me. It was Perry Kingsley.
Howard Perry?
Joanna He immediately left the man he was with and demanded to know what I was doing in that neck of the woods — and why I was in such a state. I told him I was on the way to Milton Cross hospital to see my father and that my car had broken down. I could tell by the way he looked at me that he didn't believe my story, so — in the end I told him the truth ...
Howard (*none too happy*) You told him you'd lost your licence and should never have been driving?
Joanna Yes. I told him everything, Howard. I felt I had to. He was so kind, so understanding. (*Pause*) When I finished my drink he insisted on getting me another one and whilst he was at the bar I telephoned the hospital. The news was better than I expected. I actually spoke to my father and arranged to see him the next day. (*A pause; at length*) When I returned to the table the drink was there, but there was no sign of Perry.
Howard That figures! Knowing Perry!

Joanna No, wait, Howard! It wasn't like that. He'd left a note with the barman saying — "Please wait for me, Joanna. I'll return as soon as I can" …

There is a pause

Howard Did you wait for him?
Joanna Yes.

Pause

Howard And did he return?
Joanna Yes, he did. Eventually …

The Lights fade to Black-out

During the black-out Howard exits

When the Lights come up Joanna is sitting at a table in the alcove. There is a drink in her hand and she is smoking a cigarette. The books, etc, have disappeared and the table is bare except for an ashtray. After a little while Joanna stubs out her cigarette

Perry enters wearing a coat

Joanna Perry!
Perry Sorry to have been so long, Joanna.
Joanna (*puzzled*) Where on earth have you been? What have you been doing?
Perry (*light-hearted*) Well — if you must know, I've been talking to the police.
Joanna (*stunned*) The police?
Perry Yes.
Joanna About me?
Perry No, not about you, Joanna. So relax. (*Smiling, as he unbuttons his coat*) I walked to the bungalow. I wanted to take a look at your car, see the damage you'd done, and weigh up the situation.
Joanna Why?

Perry sits at the table

Perry Why? Because I'd made up my mind to try and help you, that's why. I'd only been there five minutes when the police arrived — having been sent for by the owner of the bungalow, a Mrs Clayton.

Act II, Scene 1

Joanna (*tense; scared*) What did you tell the police?
Perry I told them what I'd already told Mrs Clayton. That I was driving a friend's car, was on my way to Milton Cross, got lost in the fog and crashed into the bungalow.
Joanna Did the police believe you?
Perry Of course they believed me! Why wouldn't they? It was routine stuff so far as they were concerned. Besides, the poor devils had more important things to worry about. There's been heaven only knows how many pile-ups on the motorway.

Joanna, enormously relieved and deeply appreciative, leans across the table and takes hold of Perry's hand

Joanna Perry, I just don't know what to say to you! I honestly don't ...
Perry Don't say anything — just keep your fingers crossed. But you're not completely out of the wood yet, Joanna. To start with — this business could cost you a bomb. Your car needs a great deal doing to it and, so far as I could tell, you haven't exactly improved the look of the bungalow.
Joanna I'm not worried about the cost Perry. That's the least of my worries. I'll pay for everything. But I am worried, *very* worried, about what I'm going to tell Howard when he gets back.
Perry (*staring at her; at length*) Howard's away?
Joanna Yes. He's in America. He's due back at the end of the month.
Perry (*thoughtfully*) That's another three weeks. (*A significant pause*) Joanna, listen! Under no circumstances must you tell Howard about tonight. For both our sakes, you mustn't confide in anyone — not a soul! You took one hell of a risk driving the car and I've stuck my neck out covering up for you ...
Joanna I realize that. But if the car's missing then Howard's going to ask questions.
Perry The car won't be missing. I'll have it back by the end of next week at the latest — that's a promise. (*After a moment's reflection*) So far as the bungalow is concerned I'll have another talk to Mrs Clayton. She struck me as being a difficult lady, but we'll come to an arrangement I'm sure. Now — what about the hospital? The fog isn't too bad at the moment.

The Lights start to fade

Joanna I've spoken to my father. He's feeling a little better. I'm seeing him tomorrow.
Perry Good. I'll drive you back to London in the Merc.

The Lights fade to Black-out

During the Black-out the books, etc. are returned to the table and the ashtray struck

Perry exits. Howard enters

The Lights gradually rise to reveal Joanna with Howard

Howard When did you next hear from Perry?
Joanna Three days later. He came to see me. He said work on the car was well in hand and I'd certainly have it back before you returned from America. Which I did, in fact.
Howard And how much did the car cost you?
Joanna Just over a thousand pounds.
Howard And the bungalow?
Joanna Perry said Mrs Clayton had already talked to a builder and the repairs would come to somewhere between fifteen and seventeen thousand. I was staggered. I had no idea I'd done that sort of damage. In fact, for a time I flatly refused to pay anything. Then one week-end, when we were down at the cottage ... (*She is near to tears*)

Pause

Howard Go on, Joanna. (*Pause*) Please go on ...
Joanna You remember the story I told you about the dog?
Howard I remember it very well.
Joanna It wasn't true. I was upset because of something Perry told me.
Howard (*with surprise*) You saw Perry, whilst we were at the cottage?
Joanna Yes. He insisted on seeing me. That's why I went for a walk that afternoon. He told me that Mrs Clayton was a trouble-maker and unless I immediately paid her fifteen thousand pounds she'd go to the police.
Howard (*puzzled*) Go to the police? About what? About Perry?
Joanna No. Not about Perry. About me.

A tense pause

She saw me, Howard.
Howard Saw you? When?
Joanna When the car crashed into the bungalow. She saw me climb out of the driver's seat and run down the lane.
Howard Did Mrs Clayton tell you that herself?
Joanna No. Perry did. I've never met Mrs Clayton.
Howard You've never met her?
Joanna No.

Act II, Scene 1

Howard Didn't it occur to you that Perry was lying?
Joanna Yes, it occurred to me. But I was too frightened to do anything about it. I was so worried, Howard. I just couldn't think straight.
Howard You should have confided in me, Joanna. You should have told me about the car, about Perry.
Joanna I wanted to, but we've had so many disagreements. And always about my driving.

Howard, stirred and compassionate, gives a little nod and finally takes hold of Joanna

Howard Yes, I know. I'm sorry.

There is an affectionate silence between them, then Howard releases her

(*At length; thoughtfully*) Joanna, the man who brought you home yesterday ... Mark Adler.
Joanna (*curiously*) Yes?
Howard Was that the first time you'd seen him?
Joanna Why, yes, of course! Why do you ask?
Howard He's a friend of Grace's. Adler has a house in Ibiza and, according to Rex Winter, Grace stayed there on one occasion.
Joanna (*after a thoughtful pause*) But that's not true. It can't be. Grace has never been to Ibiza.
Howard That's what I thought. But Winter claims to have seen her there.
Joanna He's mistaken. He must be.

The doorbell rings

Howard (*looking towards the hall*) That could be Grace now. I've been trying to get hold of her.
Joanna Wasn't she at the Board meeting?
Howard No, she wasn't! And she didn't even phone.

Joanna goes out into the hall

There is a pause during which we hear the front door opening and closing

After a moment, Joanna enters with Mark Adler who is carrying a newspaper

Joanna (*puzzled*) It's Mr Adler, Howard. He'd very much like to have a word with you.

Howard Yes, of course! Come along in, Mr Adler.
Mark I hope I'm not disturbing you?
Joanna (*to Mark*) Will you excuse me?
Mark I trust you've recovered from yesterday, Mrs Mansfield?
Joanna Yes, I have. I'm feeling much better, thank you.

Joanna exits into the conservatory

Howard Do sit down.
Mark (*shaking his head*) What I've got to say will only take a few minutes. (*Wasting no time; coming straight to the point*) Mr Mansfield, I've been reading about what happened here last night, between you and Perry Kingsley. It so happens I know Perry. I met him in Ibiza ...
Howard Is that what you wanted to tell me?
Mark No. It's about the young man who stole your wife's handbag. You may recall, I thought I'd seen him before somewhere? Well — this afternoon I suddenly remembered where it was. Perry Kingsley had a café in Ibiza and — believe it or not — that young man worked for him!

To Mark's astonishment there is hardly any reaction from Howard

Well? (*He stares at Howard, surprised and not a little disappointed*) Don't you think that's a remarkable coincidence?
Howard I do. I certainly do. But it's not the only coincidence, Mr Adler. The young man in question — Rex Winter — came to see me. He'd been questioned by the police and was frightened that my wife might bring charges against him. We talked about Perry and it was then that I learnt — much to my surprise, I might add — that you were a friend of his.
Mark I wouldn't have called Perry a friend, exactly. A friend, in my book, is someone you can trust and I certainly didn't trust Perry Kingsley. When he opened the café he talked me into lending him several pictures. Later, when the place folded, he didn't return them — claiming I'd given them to him. Needless to say, I was angry. I very nearly took him to court over it. (*A shrug*) But Perry talked his way out of it. (*Pause*) What else did — Winter did you say his name was? — tell you?
Howard He said you had a lovely villa in Ibiza and on one occasion a friend of my wife's stayed there.
Mark (*puzzled*) A friend of Mrs Mansfield's?
Howard Grace Kingsley. Perry's ex-wife.
Mark (*shaking his head*) I didn't even know Perry had been married.
Howard You've never met Mrs Kingsley?
Mark Not to my knowledge.

Act II, Scene 1

There is a pause, then Howard crosses the room, picks up a photograph, and brings it down to him

Howard (*showing him the photograph*) That's Mrs Kingsley, with my wife.

Mark studies the photograph for a moment, then shakes his head

Mark We've never met, I can assure you. And so far as I know, she's never stayed at the villa.
Howard Could she have stayed there without your knowledge?
Mark It's possible, I suppose. A Spanish couple look after the place and friends do drop in on them from time to time. But no-one's supposed to stay the night without my knowing about it.

They both move towards the hall

Maybe I should give them a ring and find out if there's any truth in Winter's story.
Howard If you do, I'd like to know what they say.

The phone rings and Howard glances across at the desk

Will you excuse me?
Mark Yes, of course, I'm sorry to have troubled you, Mr Mansfield.

Mark exits

Howard crosses to the phone

Howard (*into the phone*) Hallo? Yes? ... (*Suddenly*) Grace! Why weren't you at the Board meeting? We waited over an hour for you. ... But surely you could have telephoned. ... (*He listens to what Grace is saying*)

Joanna enters

Joanna Grace?

Howard nods to Joanna

Howard (*into the phone*) ... You sound worried, Grace. What's troubling you? ...(*A distinct pause*) I think that's a very good idea! Please do that! I shall be here all evening. (*He puts down the receiver*)
Joanna What's happened?

Howard She says she's desperately worried, and she wants to talk to me. She's calling round this evening. It sounds to me as if —— (*He breaks off*)

Mark's and Chris's voice are heard in the hall

Mark enters with Chris

Mark You've got a visitor, Mr Mansfield
Howard (*with surprise*) Why, hallo Inspector!

Mark stares at Chris suddenly realizing who he is

Mark I'm sorry, Inspector! I didn't recognize you without your beard.
Chris It happens all the time, sir. (*To Howard*) Can you and Mrs Mansfield spare a moment?
Howard Yes, by all means. (*Dismissing Mark*) Thank you, Mr Adler.

Mark smiles at Joanna and exits

Howard (*to Joanna*) This is Chief Inspector Coldwell, Joanna.
Chris (*friendly*) Mrs Mansfield ...
Howard What can I do for you, Inspector?
Chris It's not you I wanted to see, sir. I'm here because of your wife. (*To Joanna*) We've been trying to locate you, Mrs Mansfield. I thought you were in Sutton Valence.
Joanna I was. I've only just got back from there.
Chris Ah! I see. Well — anyway we've found you. No harm done.

Howard is somewhat puzzled by the Inspector's manner

Howard Sit down, Inspector.
Chris Thank you, sir.(*He sits*)
Howard Perhaps you'd care for a drink?
Chris I would, sir, very much. But — not just at the moment. (*He sits on the sofa, makes himself comfortable, then proceeds to consult notes he has made on the back of an envelope*) Mrs Mansfield, we've received certain information from the Surrey Constabulary. As I understand it, on the night of June 10th, Perry Kingsley borrowed your car and drove to Milton Cross. It was a foggy night and towards the end of the journey he took the wrong turning and crashed into the side of a bungalow ... (*He stops and looks at Joanna for confirmation*)

Joanna looks at Howard

Act II, Scene 1

Joanna (*at length; hesitantly*) That's not strictly true, Inspector.
Chris Not strictly true?
Joanna No. Perry — Mr Kingsley — didn't borrow my car ...
Chris He didn't? Then how do you account for the fact that the local police interviewed Mr Kingsley? And not only that they examined the car. (*He glances at his notes*) A Vauxhall, M496 AGY. (*He looks up*) That is your car?
Joanna Yes, that's my car. But — Perry wasn't driving it. You see, what actually happened ... (*She is momentarily lost for words*)
Chris Go on, Mrs Mansfield.
Joanna My father had a heart attack and was taken to Milton Cross hospital. Naturally I was worried. Desperately worried. Also — I was in a very difficult situation. I'd lost my licence and wasn't allowed to drive.
Howard My wife tried, without success, to get hold of a driver. In the end she did what you and I would have done under the circumstances. She drove the car herself.
Chris I see.
Howard Unfortunately, she got lost in the fog and drove headlong into a bungalow. She was terrified. The last thing she wanted was to get involved with the police ...
Chris Point taken, sir ...
Howard So she jumped out of the car, ran down the lane, and finished up having a drink in a nearby pub.
Chris Go on, Mr Mansfield.
Howard Perry Kingsley was in the bar and my wife made the fatal mistake of confiding in him. Not long afterwards ... (*He suddenly stops and moves down to the sofa*) Look! Do I have to tell you things I'm quite sure you know already?

There is an appreciable pause, then Chris tears up the envelope he is holding, and puts it in his pocket

Chris No, sir, you don't. (*He rises*) Correct me if I'm mistaken. Kingsley switched on the charm, pretended to help your wife, and finished up blackmailing her.
Howard You're not mistaken.
Chris It was your wife who tried to take the gun away from Kingsley the night he was shot. Not you, Mr Mansfield.

Howard makes no comment as Chris turns towards Joanna

What did the encounter cost you? Ten thousand pounds? Fifteen, maybe?
Joanna The best part of twenty. Some of which went to a Mrs Clayton.

Chris A Mrs Clayton? Who's Mrs Clayton?
Joanna She's the owner of the bungalow. She saw me climb out of the car and run down the lane.
Chris Did she, now? That's interesting. Who told you that? Kingsley?
Joanna Yes.
Chris There is no Mrs Clayton. The bungalow's empty. It's been empty since the owner — an old boy called Draper — died some eighteen months ago. (*He turns towards Howard again*) You've both been very frank with me, sir, so I think it's only fair that I should put my cards on the table.
Howard Cards on the table? I've been hearing that cliché all afternoon!
Chris (*smiling*) Is that so, sir?
Howard Yes — and in my experience it usually means the person in question wants something. I doubt very much whether you're an exception, Inspector.
Chris (*faintly amused*) You're quite right, sir. I'm not.
Howard Then out with it! What is it you want?
Chris Since you're kind enough to ask me. I'll tell you. (*He quickly turns and points to the picture "Flowers On A Tray"*) I'd very much like to borrow that picture.
Howard Borrow it?
Chris Yes, sir.

Pause

Howard looks at Joanna, then at Chris, puzzled

Howard (*at length*) You can borrow it, certainly.
Chris Thank you.
Howard (*curious*) But why do you wish to do so?
Chris (*evasive; yet friendly*) I'll answer that question later, sir, if I may. (*He crosses to the wall, and stands looking at the painting*)

Pause

It's a pleasant picture, I must say. Easy to live with. I was admiring it only the other day. Is it true you bought it from Perry Kingsley?
Howard (*a shade surprised*) Yes, it is.
Chris When was that, sir?
Howard Just before he emigrated. Perry had a going-away sale and we bought several things from him.

Joanna nods in agreement

Act II, Scene 2

Chris (*pleasantly*) I see. (*He smiles at both Joanna and Howard, then carefully removes the picture from the wall; pause*) You've been most helpful, sir, and you too, Mrs Mansfield. I'll return the picture as soon as possible.

The Lights start to fade

Chris exits with the picture

Black-out

Scene 2

The same. Two hours later. The window looking on to the garden is open

Mark Adler enters from the hall followed by Howard

Howard You've been remarkably quick. It's barely ten minutes since you telephoned me.
Mark I was in the car. I'm on my way to Guildford.
Howard Ah! I see. (*Pointing to the sofa*) Well — please sit down, Mr Adler.
Mark Thank you. (*He moves to the sofa and is about to sit down when he notices the wall space left by the removal of "Flowers On A Tray"*) Hallo! What's happened to the picture? Don't tell me you've sold it?
Howard No, no. We've simply lent it to someone.
Mark Not an art dealer, I hope? Never trust an art dealer. They're worse than estate agents. (*A moment*) Mr Mansfield, when I left you this afternoon I had an uneasy feeling at the back of my mind. I had the feeling — the impression if you like — that you didn't believe me. That you thought I'd lied to you.
Howard Lied to me? What about?
Mark About Mrs Kingsley.
Howard I can't imagine what gave you that impression.
Mark I've never met Mrs Kingsley, I assure you, and so far as I know I've never set eyes on her. On the other hand, I'm afraid that young man — Rex Winter — told you the truth. Mrs Kingsley did stay at my place. I've spoken to the couple who look after the villa. Apparently, it was Perry Kingsley's doing. He told them I'd given permission for both he and a friend to stay here.
Howard Which wasn't true?
Mark Which most certainly wasn't true!
Howard But why would Perry do that?
Mark I can't imagine why he did it. Ibiza's not exactly short of hotels.

Howard (*thoughtfully*) Well — thank you for putting the record straight.
Mark That chap Winter's got the cheek of the devil. He came to see me this evening, just as we were closing the gallery. He said he was hard up and now that Perry was out of circulation he was looking for a job.
Howard I trust you offered him one?
Mark But of course! I offered to put him on the payroll straight away. Providing he switched from handbags to impressionists.

Howard laughs

The doorbell rings

Mark looks towards the hall

Howard Excuse me ...

Howard goes into the hall

Pause

Howard and Chris are heard off stage

Howard returns accompanied by Chris. Chris carries the painting "Flowers On A Tray".

Chris I'm returning your picture, sir. Thank you for lending it to us.(*He puts the picture down*)

Mark, a shade surprised, looks at the picture, then at Chris

(*To Mark*) Good-evening, sir.
Mark Good-evening, Inspector.
Howard We've just been talking about Kingsley, Inspector. How is he?
Chris Much the same, sir. But it's early days.
Mark Is he conscious?
Chris Hardly ever, and then not for long, unfortunately.
Mark I have a house in Ibiza and used to drop into his café from time to time.

Chris nods

Smooth sort of chap. Could be very amusing though. Usually at other people's expense. (*He glances at his watch as he turns towards the hall*) Can't say I'd really trust him.

Act II, Scene 2   51

Howard joins Mark

Mark Don't bother, Mr Mansfield. I can see myself out.

Mark exits

Pause

Howard You've met Adler before?
Chris Yes. About six months ago. His gallery was broken into.
Howard I remember reading about it.

Chris picks up "Flowers On A Tray" with the intention of hanging it

I'll deal with the picture later, Inspector.
Chris Oh. Thank you, sir. (*He places the picture by the side of the sofa*) I won't keep you. And thank you again — and Mrs Mansfield — for your co-operation. (*He starts to leave*)
Howard I hope you found what you were looking for?

Chris slowly turns, faintly surprised by the question

Chris No, sir. I'm afraid we didn't.
Howard What exactly were you looking for? Or shouldn't I ask that question?
Chris (*a moment*) I see no reason why you shouldn't ask it. (*Pause*) We were looking for a letter.
Howard A letter?
Chris A most important letter. I had a hunch — I'm afraid I get them from time to time — that it was hidden behind that picture. Unfortunately I was wrong.
Howard Why that picture?
Chris It once belonged to Perry Kingsley.
Howard And Perry had the letter? Is that what you are saying?
Chris (*with good natured exasperation*) To be honest, we don't know whether he had it or not. There was certainly a rumour to that effect. But then, there's been so many rumours concerning the whereabouts of that wretched letter.
Howard Who wrote the letter, Inspector?
Chris I'm afraid I can't tell you. Except to say, the man in question ought to have had more sense. The letter was sent to an Italian girl. A well-known model, as I understand it. Unfortunately it never reached her. (*He moves nearer the hall, then stops*) One thing's for sure! If that letter's ever made public, the world press — and I mean the world press — will have a field-day. Believe me, we've got to find that letter, come hell or high water!

Chris exits into the hall followed by Howard

There is a definite pause

Hilary enters from the garden. She is wearing outdoor clothes

Pause

Howard returns and is astonished to find Hilary waiting for him

Howard Why, hallo, Hilary!
Hilary (*tense, nervous; without thinking*) May I come in?
Howard (*amused*) You are in!
Hilary I've been waiting in the garden. I heard voices and I didn't want to ... Howard, are you free? I'd very much like to talk to you.
Howard Yes, of course. But I thought you were in the wilds of Yorkshire chatting up Roger's constituents.
Hilary (*moving down to him*) Roger's got to be in the House on Thursday so we shan't get away until the weekend. (*After a nervous hesitation*) Are you alone? I mean — is Joanna around?
Howard No, she's with her mother. What is it, Hilary? What's worrying you?
Hilary Howard, I've got a problem and I'm hoping you may be able to help me.
Howard If I can, I will. You know that.
Hilary I've been trying to get hold of Grace Kingsley. I've tried the office, I've tried her flat, I've telephoned several of her friends, but no-one seems to know where she is ...
Howard I know how you feel! The office spent the best part of the afternoon trying to locate her.
Hilary Wasn't she at the Board meeting?
Howard (*annoyed*) No, she wasn't.
Hilary That's most unlike Grace. (*There is a tiny pause, then she turns from him, disappointed*) Well, obviously you can't help me ...
Howard No, wait! I may be able to help you. Grace rang me. She's calling round this evening.
Hilary Oh! Well — please ask her to phone me. I must talk to her, Howard.
Howard (*with curiousity*) Yes, of course.
Hilary It's important, Howard. Very important!
Howard I've got the message. (*Smiling*) I'll see she gets yours.

Hilary moves to go. Howard stops her

Act II, Scene 2   53

It's none of my business, but why do you wish to see Grace? As I recall, the two of you have never been particularly friendly.
Hilary (*evasively*) I just want to talk to her about something, that's all.
Howard Something to do with the office?
Hilary No, no! It's nothing to do with the office. (*Concerned*) It's Roger ...
Howard Roger's in trouble?
Hilary Not yet. But he will be — in terrible trouble — unless I do something about it.
Howard Unless *you* do something about it? (*Curiously*) What's Roger done, Hilary?
Hilary He hasn't done anything. At least ... (*There is a slight hesitation before she finally decides to confide in him*) Four days ago — last Monday to be exact — Perry Kingsley came to see me.
Howard Perry did! Was Perry a friend of yours?
Hilary No. I hardly knew him. I'd only met him once and that was years ago at a party.
Howard Go on ...
Hilary He said he had some photographs which he was about to offer to one of the tabloids. But first — he wanted me to take a look at them. (*Pause*) They were photographs of Roger. To say I was surprised by the photographs would be the understatement of the year! I was staggered, Howard, and very badly shaken ...
Howard Why were you shaken? Because of the way he looked?

Hilary hesitates

Because of the clothes Roger was wearing?
Hilary (*softly*) Yes ...

Pause

Howard Where were the photographs taken, do you know?
Hilary I imagine at some wretched transvestite club, or other, if that's what they're called.
Howard Did you tell Roger you'd seen the photographs?
Hilary No.
Howard Why not?
Hilary I couldn't face him. I just couldn't! I've felt so angry! Angry, and yet at the same time, sorry for the poor fool. Can you imagine what would happen if the photographs were published? His career — everything he's worked for — would be in jeopardy.
Howard What did Perry say when he showed you the photographs?
Hilary He said very little, but it was obvious he was hoping I'd buy them from him. (*A moment*) I was out of my depth, Howard. I just didn't know what to do or say.

Howard What did you do?
Hilary In the end I said I'd give the matter thought and get back to him. Forty-eight hours later, to my astonishment, I read that he'd been shot and was in intensive care. At first, I must confess, I felt a sense of relief. Then it dawned on me that, not withstanding what happened to Perry, the photographs were still in existence.
Howard Go on, Hilary.
Hilary Late last night, I went to an address Perry had given me. An apartment block in Pimlico. There was a resident porter and I did my best to talk him into letting me into Perry's flat. (*Shaking her head*) He made it quite clear it was more than his job was worth. He said an Inspector Coldwell had visited the apartment more than once and had left instructions that no-one had to be admitted.

Howard nods

However, just as I was leaving, he suggested I get in touch with Mrs Kingsley.
Howard Grace? Why Grace?
Hilary He said Mrs Kingsley had access to the flat and was constantly dropping in.
Howard Was Grace living with Perry?
Hilary I think she must have been.

The doorbell rings and they both hear it

Howard hesitates, then quickly exits

As Hilary stands staring into the hall. There is the sound of the door opening and closing

Howard's and Grace's voices are heard

Howard (*off*) Come along in! I'm glad you've made it. What's happened, Grace? You sounded dreadful on the phone.
Grace (*off; a distinct note of urgency in her voice*) We've got to talk, Howard. It's important. Is Joanna with you?

Howard enters with Grace who is carrying a briefcase

Howard Joanna's not here. Her mother's not well, I'm afraid.

Grace is staring at Hilary, surprised to see her, and not at all pleased

Act II, Scene 2   55

Grace (*cold; unfriendly*) Why, hallo, Hilary!
Hilary Thank goodness, you've come, Grace! I've been trying to get hold of you. I've telephoned everywhere.
Grace Yes, well — I'm afraid we can't talk now. There are things I must discuss with Howard. Important things.
Hilary Grace, please listen to me! If only for a moment! I've got a problem and you're the only one that can help me.
Grace We've all got problems, Hilary. I must talk to Howard, privately. It's urgent! So please leave us …
Howard I think you'd better go, Hilary.
Hilary No! (*To Grace*) I've been trying to get in touch with you since nine o'clock last night. I'm desperate, Grace! I really am! I need your help!

Pause

Grace What makes you think I can help you?
Howard Hilary has been told that you have access to Perry's apartment and she was wondering whether you would …
Grace What business is that of Hilary's? (*To Hilary*) I'm sorry, I can't help you! I've got to see Howard alone! Now! This minute! So please leave us!

Grace sees the expression on Hilary's face

(*Relenting slightly*) I'll phone you. I'll talk to you later this evening …

Howard takes Hilary by the arm and leads her towards the window

Howard I'll have a word with Grace. Come along, my dear.

Howard and Hilary exit

Grace puts the briefcase down and sinks into the nearest armchair. She looks tired and depressed as she buries her head in her hands

Pause

Howard enters and stands for a moment

Pause

Grace suddenly looks up

Grace I'm sorry.

Howard What is it, Grace?
Grace I'm frightened, Howard.
Howard Frightened? Frightened of what?
Grace I'm frightened of what might happen to me.
Howard Why should anything happen to you? (*Pause*) Is this something to do with Perry?

Grace nods

Have you been living with him since he left Ibiza?
Grace Yes. But first, before anything else, I must tell you about last night. I went to the hospital in the hope of seeing Perry. They wouldn't let me see him but just as I was leaving I got talking to one of the nurses. She said Perry had tried, more than once, to tell them something about someone called Merc. or Mark. (*Shaking her head*) I've never heard of anyone by that name, but on the way home it occurred to me that the nurse was mistaken and that Perry had been simply trying to say something about his car.
Howard His car?
Grace He's got a new Mercedes and he's for ever talking about his Merc. as he calls it.
Howard Go on, Grace.
Grace I drove round to the apartment and questioned the porter. He said Perry's car had been returned to the garage and he gave me the keys. I had a feeling, I don't quite know why, that Perry wasn't worried about the car itself, but about something in the car.
Howard That makes sense.

Grace rises and picks up the briefcase

Grace I found this. It was hidden in a compartment at the back of the boot. (*She puts the briefcase down on the table*)

Howard moves down to Grace, his eyes on the case

Pause

Howard The lock's broken.
Grace Yes, I know. I broke it.

Howard looks at her

I wanted to know what was in the case. I had to know, Howard!
Howard Why did you *have* to know?

Act II, Scene 2   57

Grace I wanted to find out what Perry was up to. For some time now I've suspected that he was no longer a wheeler dealer but was into something far more sinister. And I was right, Howard! Take a look at these photographs.

Grace opens the briefcase and produces several large photographs which she hands to Howard

Grace Believe it or not, that's Hilary's husband.

Howard stares at the photographs

Pause

Howard Hilary told me about these. That's why she came to see me. (*Putting the photographs down*) What else is in the case?
Grace There are other photographs. The most appalling photographs — mostly of well known people. I can't imagine how they were taken. (*She is searching the case*) There's a dozen tapes or more, a diary of Perry's, and several videos. Oh! And there's a letter addressed to someone in Milan …

Grace produces an airmail letter and an important looking diary. To her surprise Howard immediately takes the letter from her and carefully examines the envelope

Pause

Howard It looks to me, as if this letter's been opened, at some point. (*He looks up*) Did you open it, Grace?
Grace No. (*Adamant; shaking her head*) No, I didn't. It must have been Perry.

Howard realizes that she is telling him the truth and, after a second glance at the letter, he puts it in his pocket

Howard What's in the diary?
Grace I haven't looked at it.
Howard What about the videos you mentioned? Have you seen them?
Grace No. After looking at the photographs I couldn't face it. I've listened to the tapes though. They're mostly telephone conversations between Perry and — various people …
Howard Joanna being one of them?
Grace Yes. Joanna being one of them. (*Pause*) He was blackmailing her, Howard.

Howard I know. She told me.
Grace (*unable to conceal a note of desperation*) I'm worried! I really am! I wish to God I'd never gone near the car. What am I going to do with these things? I daren't take them to the police.
Howard Why daren't you?
Grace They'll question me. They'll want to know about my relationship with Perry. Whether I am involved in what he was doing.
Howard Were you involved?
Grace No, of course not! But I have a horrible feeling Perry made use of me.
Howard In what way?

There is a rather awkward silence between them

Grace, you came here because you realized you were out of your depth and needed help. It's possible, just possible, that I may be able to help you. But I can't — I won't, in fact — unless you're completely honest with me

Pause

Grace Shortly before Perry left Ibiza I had a phone call from him. He said he was beginning to hate the island, and was desperately anxious to see me again. Well — you know me, Howard, when it comes to Perry. Within an hour of putting the phone down, I was packed and ready to go. (*Pause*) Perry was certainly pleased to see me, but from the moment I arrived I had the feeling that I was there for a specific reason. Also, he asked me, more than once, not to mention my visit to anyone. Which I found strange.
Howard Where did you stay in Ibiza?
Grace Perry had arranged for us to stay at a villa. A beautiful place, which belonged to a friend of his.
Howard Did he tell you who the friend was?
Grace No, he didn't. He simply said he was a wealthy man who had several homes on the Continent. (*Pause*) The morning I was leaving, Perry asked me to deliver a small parcel — a cassette — to a shop in Kensington. I delivered the cassette and twenty-four hours later I read that the woman who owned the shop had committed suicide. (*Tensely*) Perry was blackmailing her, Howard. I'm sure he was! Which means I was partly responsible for what happened …
Howard That's nonsense, Grace! Put that thought out of your head. You didn't know what was on the tape. You'd no idea. (*Pause*) Does anyone else know you've got the briefcase?
Grace No …
Howard What about the porter? Did he see you leave the garage?
Grace I don't think so, but he might have done.

Act II, Scene 2   59

Howard remains silent for a little while. He is like a man faced with a problem and trying to decide on a course of action

Howard (*urgently; having reached a decision*) Grace, I'll tell you what I want you to do! Leave the briefcase with me and go back to your flat. Don't answer the door and don't make any phone calls. Is that clear?
Grace Yes, but ——
Howard Absolutely clear?
Grace Yes ...
Howard I'll phone you first thing tomorrow morning.

Howard and Grace exit

A moment later Howard returns, crosses to the table, quickly gathers up the photographs Hilary wanted and takes them down to the desk. Having placed the photographs in a drawer he picks up the phone and dials

Pause

(*Into the phone*) ... This is Howard Mansfield. Could I speak to Chief Inspector Coldwell? (*Pause*) I see ... Well — please contact the Inspector and ask him to get in touch with me as soon as possible ... Thank you. (*He puts the phone down and moves back to the table. He hesitates for a second or two then, obviously curious, he decides to take a look at the other photographs in the briefcase*)

Pause

Howard is distinctly shaken by the photographs he finds. There is a tense pause before he quickly returns them to the briefcase and picks up the diary. He flicks through the pages of the diary and is about to place it in the briefcase when something arouses his attention. He studies the diary

Joanna enters from the hall

Howard (*with surprise*) Joanna! (*He puts the diary down and moves towards her*) How are things with your mother? Is she any better?
Joanna No, I'm afraid she isn't.
Howard Oh! I'm sorry. What does the doctor say?
Joanna He doesn't seem to think it's serious, but I'm going to stay with her, Howard. Tonight, at any rate.
Howard Yes, of course. If there's anything I can do ...
Joanna I'm afraid there isn't, darling. (*A shade flustered*) I'll be with you in a minute. I'm just going to collect a few things.

Joanna exits

Howard picks up the diary and moves down to the sofa. He sits on the sofa, absorbed in the diary

Joanna returns carrying a night-dress, a make-up box, and a dressing-gown

Joanna What's happened about Grace? Did she call round?
Howard Yes. You've only just missed her.
Joanna What was all the histrionics about? You said she sounded dreadful on the phone?
Howard She's been living with Perry since he left Ibiza ...
Joanna That doesn't surprise me ...
Howard And because of that, she's frightened the police might think she was an accomplice of his. (*A moment*) Joanna, there's something I want to ask you. That night — the night you bumped in to Perry in the pub.
Joanna Yes?
Howard If I remember rightly, you said there was a man with him?
Joanna Yes, there was.
Howard Can you remember what the man looked like?
Joanna (*puzzled*) No, I'm afraid I can't ... I didn't take any notice of him.
Howard But you saw him?
Joanna Yes, I saw him. I must have done. But I really haven't the slightest idea what he looks like.
Howard Think, Joanna. Cast your mind back, if you can. Was he a young man?

Pause

Joanna I have a feeling he wasn't very old, but — I honestly don't know. I was very distressed at the time, almost desperate ...
Howard Yes, I appreciate that. But — was he tall? Dark? Fair? Had he a beard?
Joanna I'm sorry, Howard. I just can't remember anything about him. If I said otherwise I'd only mislead you.
Howard (*a moment; disappointed*) Yes, all right, Joanna. (*He crosses to the desk and puts the diary down*)

The phone rings

(*Answering the phone*) Yes, speaking. (*Pause*) Oh, hallo, Inspector! Thank you for ringing. You'll be interested to ... (*He suddenly stops speaking*)

There is a long pause. Howard is listening intently to what is being said to him

Act II, Scene 3

Joanna, struck by his change of manner, joins him at the desk

(*Quietly, into the phone*) Yes. I shall be here ... (*He slowly puts the phone down*)

Joanna What is it, Howard? What's happened?
Howard That was Inspector Coldwell. He's at the hospital. Perry's dead. He died about half an hour ago.

Black-out

Scene 3

The same. An hour later

The telephone is ringing

Howard comes out of the dining-room and crosses to the desk. He picks up the phone

There is the unmistakable sound of the front doorbell

Howard hesitates and looks towards the hall

Howard (*into the phone*) ... Just hold on, please ... (*He puts the receiver down on the desk*)

Howard exits into the hall

Pause

Howard's and Chris's voices are heard in the hall

Howard enters accompanied by Chris

Will you excuse me? I'm on the phone ...(*He indicates the sofa and returns to the desk; into the phone*) ... Oh, hallo, Hilary! ... I'm sorry, my dear, I can't talk now. ... (*About to put the phone down*) What's that? ... I've found what you were looking for. Call round tomorrow morning and you can pick them up ...(*He rings off and moves down to Chris*) I'm sorry about that. Do sit down.

Chris looks towards the sofa, finally deciding on an armchair

Chris I understand you wished to see me?
Howard Yes, but first — tell me about Perry Kingsley. What happened, exactly?

Chris He had a relapse late this afternoon and never recovered. It happened quite suddenly, as I understand it.
Howard Was anyone with Perry?
Chris Yes. A nurse and the young doctor who'd been looking after him. Incidentally, Kingsley talked to the doctor last night. He told him the shooting incident was an accident and that Mrs Mansfield wasn't to blame.
Howard I'm relieved to hear that. But — why do that, I wonder?
Chris I don't know. (*Shaking his head*) Maybe he had a premonition. Maybe he knew he wasn't going to make it. (*A pause*) Now — what's your problem, Mr Mansfield? Why did you wish to see me? (*He stares at Howard with curiousity*)
Howard I haven't got a problem. But I have got something which will interest you. Very much so, unless I'm mistaken.

Howard takes the letter out of his pocket and hands it to Chris, who immediately examines it

Pause

Howard Is it the letter? The one you've been looking for?
Chris (*at length*) It looks remarkably like it ... (*He produces a card from his wallet and carefully compares the writing on the card with that on the envelope*)

A long pause

Yes, it is! It's the same handwriting! (*He looks at Howard*) It's obviously been opened by someone ...
Howard Yes — but not by me.

Pause

Chris How long have you had this?
Howard About an hour. I phoned your office immediately I received it.
Chris How did you come by it? Who gave you the letter?

An uneasy pause

Howard I hope you won't take offence, Inspector. But, for a variety of reasons, I don't wish to answer that question.
Chris No, sir?
Howard No. Not at the moment, at any rate.

Chris stares at Howard, then suddenly smiles

Act II, Scene 3

Chris Well — I shan't take offence, sir. How can I? You've taken a load off my mind and I'm more than grateful. (*He looks at the letter again, then places it in his pocket*) In fact, in my book, this calls for a celebration. Some time back you offered me a drink? May I take you up on that?

Howard is puzzled. He was expecting a barrage of questioning

Howard Er — yes. Yes, by all means.

Howard crosses to the drinks cabinet and prepares a couple of drinks, one of which he takes down to Chris. Chris takes the drink from him, and raises his glass. Howard, still puzzled, makes the same gesture. They drink

A long pause

Chris (*matter of fact*) Was the letter in the briefcase, sir?
Howard (*taken aback*) You know about the briefcase?
Chris I know that Mrs Kingsley called on you this evening and that she was carrying a briefcase. I also know that when she left here, some little time later, she was empty-handed.
Howard How do you know that? Have you people been keeping an eye on Grace — Mrs Kingsley?
Chris Yes, sir. We've been keeping an eye on her. It's my opinion, Mrs Kingsley worked for her ex-husband. That she was in fact an associate of his.
Howard You're on the wrong track, Inspector. Grace was certainly besotted with Perry, but never, at any time, did she work for him.

Chris looks at Howard, steadily

Chris I'm pleased to hear that.

They both continue with their drinks, then Chris finally puts his glass down and rises

Now — if you don't mind — I'd like to take a look at Mrs Kingsley's briefcase. I imagine you still have it?
Howard Yes, I have it, but it's not Mrs Kingsley's. It belonged to Perry. Grace found it in the boot of his car.
Chris What's in the case?
Howard Mostly photographs and tapes ...
Chris Tapes of what? Telephone conversations?
Howard Yes. (*He takes the briefcase out of the desk cupboard and places it on the table*)

Chris looks at the case, indicating the broken lock

Chris Did you do this, sir?
Howard No. Grace did. The case was locked and she was curious about the contents.
Chris Was she also curious about the letter?
Howard Yes. But not to the extent of opening it.
Chris You're sure about that?
Howard I'm quite sure.

Chris gives a little nod, opens the case, and takes out several of the photographs

Pause

Chris (*under his breath, slowly examining the photographs*) My God! People ... (*Long pause*) You've seen these, I take it?
Howard Yes, I've seen them.
Chris Do you recognize any of these people?
Howard I think we both do, Inspector.

Chris gives a little nod and continues studying the photographs, finally looking up

Chris Was there anything else in the briefcase?
Howard (*surprised by the question*) Anything else?
Chris Have you, or Mrs Kingsley, removed anything from the case?
Howard (*a brief hesitation*) Yes, I have. (*He crosses to the desk and picks up the diary*) There was this diary.
Chris (*instantly curious*) It's Perry Kingsley's?
Howard Yes, it's Perry's. And it makes interesting reading.

Chris immediately returns the photographs to the briefcase and gives the diary his attention. There is a long pause whilst Chris — watched by Howard — examines the diary

Chris Makes interesting reading did you say? That's an understatement if ever I've heard one! (*He closes the diary*) I'll examine this later.
Howard Would it be possible for me to hold on to the diary, Inspector?
Chris Hold on to it?
Howard Just for the next twenty-four hours?
Chris (*after a moment's thought*) No, sir. I'm afraid it wouldn't. But why do you wish to do that?

Act II, Scene 3   65

Howard It's just that — well, to be frank — I think I can make better use of it than you, Inspector.
Chris (*amused*) Is that so, sir? Well, I'm sorry I can't help you (*Pause; almost second thoughts*) It's possible, I suppose, — just possible — that we might be able to supply you with a copy.
Howard It would have to look like the genuine article. The real thing.

Pause

Chris We'll see what we can do, sir.
Howard Thank you.
Chris You say the briefcase was in Kingsley's car?
Howard Yes, and Grace was stunned when she opened it. She just didn't know what to do. In the end she consulted me. Would she have done that, if she'd been an associate of Perry's?
Chris Point taken! No, sir, she wouldn't. (*A thoughtful pause*) Kingsley must have had the case with him the night he came here, the night he was shot.
Howard He must have done. (*At length*) Come to think of it, he was on his way to a meeting.

Pause

The significance of Howard's remark suddenly dawns on Chris

Chris On his way to a meeting?
Howard He told my wife that.
Chris Did he? Did he indeed! (*Giving the matter thought*) Do you know what I think? I think Kingsley was not only on his way to a meeting, he was about to report to someone.
Howard What are you suggesting? That Perry wasn't a free agent?
Chris Thanks to the tabloids, the blackmailing fraternity have never had it so good. Blackmail's big business these days. Every project is carefully organized and masterminded.
Howard And Perry wasn't in that league?
Chris I doubt it. I doubt it very much. I think, in the end, someone took over from him. Someone a great deal cleverer. (*He picks up the briefcase, preparing to leave*) Still — not to worry. We'll nail the son-of-a-bitch sooner or later.
Howard I hope you do, Inspector. And I only wish I could help you.

They are both moving towards the hall when Chris suddenly hesitates

Pause

Chris Did you mean what you said just now, sir? That you'd like to help us?
Howard Why, yes. Of course ...
Chris Even if we asked you to take a calculated risk?
Howard In publishing we take calculated risks almost every day.
Chris That's not the sort of risk I have in mind.
Howard What have you in mind, Inspector?
Chris (*at length*) Well, first of all, I'd like you to come down to the station, sir.
Howard Now? Straightaway?
Chris No. In about an hour's time. I want you to meet a colleague of mine. He'll explain certain things to you.

Pause

Howard Very well. In about an hour.
Chris Thank you. (*Once again he is about to leave, then stops*) Oh! By the way, Mr Mansfield, the other day I happened to notice the sports jacket you were wearing.
Howard The sports jacket?
Chris Yes, sir. The grey one. Perhaps you'd be good enough to wear it when you come down to the station.
Howard My grey sports jacket?
Chris That's right, sir. We'll expect you in about an hour.

The Lights fade

Scene 4

The same. The following morning

It is a warm morning and the window is open

Howard is at his desk looking at Hilary. Hilary stands nearby. Howard is without a jacket and is on the verge of handing Hilary a large envelope. The envelope contains the photographs of her husband

Hilary I just don't know what to say to you, Howard. I'll never be able to repay you for what you've done.
Howard You can repay me by forgetting the entire incident. Remember — I know nothing about these photographs. I've never even seen them! You understand?

Hilary nods

Act II, Scene 4

Howard rises, moves round the desk, and hands her the envelope

Howard Take it easy with your husband, Hilary. Whatever you do, don't lose your temper. Roger's a kind, caring sort of chap. Well liked by his constituents. Try and remember that fact.
Hilary Tea and sympathy? Is that what you prescribe?
Howard Knowing Roger, I'm not sure about the tea. But a little understanding might not be such a bad idea.

The doorbell rings and Howard glances at his watch

I'm expecting a visitor. Let him in, Hilary and ask him to wait.
Hilary Yes, of course. And thank you again, Howard, for everything. (*She kisses him*)

Hilary exits

Howard looks towards the hall, then quickly exits into the conservatory

A brief pause

Hilary enters with Rex Winter. He has an air of confidence about him and is somewhat better dressed than the last time we saw him

Rex is surprised to find the room deserted

Hilary Mr Mansfield will be with you shortly.

Rex stares at her for a second or two, then nods

Hilary exits

There is an appreciable pause before Howard returns. He is now wearing his grey sports jacket

Rex faces him

Rex I had a message — an urgent message — saying you wished to see me.
Howard (*pleasantly, yet with authority*) That's right. Thank you for coming. Sit down, Winter. (*He moves to his desk and indicates the chair facing him*) I take it you've heard about Perry?
Rex Yes, I heard last night. I thought the poor devil was on the mend.
Howard I thought so too.

Pause

Rex hesitates, then sits

Rex Why do you wish to see me?
Howard We'll come to that in a minute.
Rex Whatever the reason I trust it won't take long. I have a busy day ahead of me and I'm leaving for Australia at the end of the week.
Howard Australia? How did that come about?
Rex I have a friend on the *Sydney Telegraph*. I sent him samples of my work and he's asked to see me.
Howard Who's paying for the trip?
Rex The paper's paying for me to go out there.
Howard That's very generous of them. Still — I'm not surprised, your work's very good, Winter.
Rex (*flattered; yet puzzled*) Thank you. But when have you seen my work? I don't recall showing you any photographs.
Howard I've seen the photographs you sold Perry Kingsley. In fact, I've got one or two of them here.

Howard takes several photographs out of a drawer and spreads them across the desk

Rex stares at them in amazement

Rex How did you get hold of these? I've done my nut trying to find them.
Howard Grace Kingsley came across them. They were in a briefcase in the boot of Perry's car. He was obviously taking them somewhere the night he called on my wife.

A *moment*

Rex Was there anything else in the briefcase?
Howard Yes. Several photographs, various tapes, a diary of Perry's and an important looking letter. The letter, together with the tapes, etc, are with Chief Inspector Coldwell. He hasn't seen the diary.
Rex Why not?
Howard I wanted you to see it first.

Howard takes a replica of Perry's diary out of a drawer

Rex Why me? What makes you think I'd be interested in Perry's diary?
Howard (*opening the diary*) You're mentioned in it.
Rex I am?

Act II, Scene 4   69

Howard Yes; more than once. For instance, this is what he wrote about you some time back. (*Reading*) "Had a long talk with Winter and finally offered him a job, which — to my amazement — he turned down. What's got into the fool?" (*He looks at Rex*) Do you recall that offer?
Rex Vaguely. He wanted me to work for him full time.
Howard And you refused?
Rex Yes. When I questioned him about the job it sounded to me like blackmail and I didn't wish to get involved.
Howard But surely, you were involved? You were already supplying him with photographs.
Rex I sold Perry photographs from time to time, but what use he made of them ... (*He hesitates*)
Howard Was no concern of yours?
Rex Exactly!

Howard studies Rex for a second or two before consulting the diary again

Howard Here's another entry which will interest you. (*Reading*) "A foul night, patches of fog everywhere. Drove down to Milton Cross for a final meeting with Norman Ryder. The meeting turned out to be a very pleasant surprise. It looks as if we're going to do a deal after all." (*He stops and looks up*)

Rex rises. He appears concerned by the extract and attempts to cover up his feelings with a display of irritation

Rex What's that got to do with me? I fail to see what you're getting at!
Howard I was hoping you might be able to elaborate ...
Rex Elaborate? On what?
Howard On the Milton Cross incident. What exactly was Perry up to? And who's this man Ryder?
Rex (*not looking at him*) I haven't the slightest idea.
Howard There's several references to him in the diary.

Rex makes no comment

Perry never mentioned him?
Rex Never.
Howard (*not convinced*) You're sure?
Rex (*on edge*) Of course I'm sure! The name Ryder means nothing to me. (*He moves towards the window*) I should forget Perry Kingsley if I were you. After all, he's dead. There's not point in digging up the past.

Howard Is that what you'll tell the Inspector when he questions you?
Rex (*taken aback*) Question me? Inspector Coldwell?
Howard Yes.
Rex Why on earth should Coldwell question me?
Howard The police are still interested in Perry Kingsley and the various contacts he made. They've a list of people they want to interview.
Rex And I'm on the list?
Howard I shall be surprised if you're not.
Rex Well, whether I'm on the list or not — Chief Inspector Coldwell can get lost! I'm answering no more questions! Now, if you'll excuse me.
Howard I wouldn't get too difficult with the police if I were you, Winter. They could very easily hold up your Australian trip.

Howard's statement makes an immediate impact on Rex

Rex (*with alarm*) Hold up my trip? What do you mean?
Howard I mean what I say. The police could hold you up indefinitely if they feel like it.
Rex (*at length; with concern*) There's nothing I can tell the police about Perry Kingsley that I haven't already told them.
Howard In which case, all you have to do is keep a civil tongue in your head and repeat your story.

An uneasy pause

Rex (*moving nearer the window*) You could be right, I suppose. The police can be bloody difficult if they want to be.
Howard Meanwhile, if something new occurs to you — which it might — don't hesitate to tell the Inspector about it.
Rex I'll try and remember to do that.
Howard I would if I were you.

Rex exits into the garden

Howard watches his departure. He finally crosses the room and opens the conservatory door

Pause

Chris enters

Chris Your little talk didn't seem to get you very far.
Howard On the contrary. It got me a great deal further than I expected.

Act II, Scene 4   71

Chris Indeed? I'm glad to hear it.
Howard What's your opinion of Winter?
Chris He reminds me of a car salesman I once knew. When he was telling the truth you thought he was lying and when he was lying you believed every word he said.
Howard Do you believe the Australian story?
Chris I'm inclined to. But I'll check with the newspaper. What's your feeling?
Howard There's no doubt Winter wants to forget Perry and make a fresh start. But I doubt very much whether the *Sydney Telegraph* are behind him.
Chris Then who is? I hardly think he's paying for the trip himself.

Pause

I spent the best part of last night reading the diary. It's not going to win the Booker prize, but by George I couldn't put it down.
Howard Had you heard of Norman Ryder before you'd read the diary?
Chris Yes, we first heard of him about a year ago. But we still haven't the slightest idea who he is. All we know is: he uses various names — one of which is Ryder — and he's been responsible for a considerable number of suicides both here and on the Continent.

Pause

Howard It's none of my business, Inspector, I realize that, but ——
Chris Go on, sir ...
Howard Apart from the diary, did you by any chance, read the letter? The all important letter?
Chris No, I'm afraid I didn't. It went straight to Scotland Yard.
Howard Then you've no idea what was in it?
Chris (*smiling*) I didn't say that, sir. (*Pause*) I know who wrote the letter and I've a pretty good idea of what was in it. But don't ask me to pursue the subject, it's more than my job's worth. However, one thing I will say. We've got some remarkably clever people in this country, make no mistake about that! But when it comes to dealing with their private affairs, I never fail to be amazed by their stupidity. Why on earth they don't take a lesson from ... (*His words fade away, his eyes are suddenly drawn to the open window*)

Rex appears from the garden. He looks distressed and in obvious pain as he holds on to the curtains. There are traces of blood on his hands and face

Howard My God, what's happened? (*He rushes towards the window*)

Chris I'll call an ambulance!

Chris quickly moves to the phone and starts dialling

Howard (*attempting to take hold of Rex*) Let me help you!

A tense pause. Then Rex releases his hold on the curtains and literally falls into Howard's arms. It is then — and only then — that we see a knife that has been plunged into his back

Black-out

Scene 5

The same. Several hours later

Mark Adler is sitting on the sofa watching Howard. Howard wears the grey sports jacket and is at the drinks cabinet, mixing himself a drink

Howard Are you sure you won't join me in a drink?
Mark Yes, I'm quite sure, thank you.

Howard finishes mixing his whisky and soda and takes it down to the desk

Howard (*sitting at the desk*) Now — tell me about the book you're thinking of writing.
Mark A few weeks ago I wrote an article on the National Gallery. It was well received and I suddenly had the bright idea of writing a book. I've written about twenty thousand words and I was wondering …
Howard (*smiling*) And you'd like me to take a look at what you've written. Is that it?
Mark That's it, exactly! I want to make sure I'm not wasting my time.
Howard No problem. Send me the material and I'll read it straightaway.
Mark Thank you.

The phone rings

Howard Excuse me (*He picks up the phone; into the phone*) Howard Mansfield … Oh! … Hallo, Inspector! … (*A slight pause*) Yes, I have, but go ahead. … No, please go ahead. … (*An appreciable pause*) … I see. … I understand. … Thank you for letting me know. (*He rings off, glances at his watch and then looks at Mark*) That was Chief Inspector Coldwell, he's keeping me posted on Rex Winter.

Act II, Scene 5

Mark Why Winter?
Howard Winter came to see me this morning. On leaving here someone tried to kill him.
Mark Good God! What happened?
Howard He'd just finishing making a phone call when a man rushed into the garden and stuck a knife in him.
Mark Did Winter recognize the man?
Howard I don't think so, but I'm not sure.
Mark How is Winter?
Howard He's had an operation and so far so good. The doctors are pretty confident he's going to be all right. But then, they said the same thing about Perry Kingsley.

Pause

Mark Tell me: do the police think this business with Winter had anything to do with Perry?
Howard I'm not sure what they think, they haven't confided in me. But why do you ask?
Mark I ask because, although Perry's dead, the police are still questioning people about him.
Howard Have they questioned you?
Mark No, they haven't. Not yet. But a journalist friend of mine who barely knew him, was questioned for over an hour yesterday morning. (*Shaking his head*) Why? Why question her about a small time operator like Perry Kingsley?
Howard Perry wasn't just a small time operator. Although that was the impression he gave people.
Mark It was certainly the impression he gave me.
Howard Perry was a blackmailer. He took photographs and gathered information about people — then proceeded to blackmail them. If they refused to co-operate, he contacted the tabloids. Perry was doing well until it suddenly dawned on him he was getting out of his depth and could no longer control his affairs. In the end, he had no alternative but to sell out.
Mark Sell out?
Howard To one of the big boys. A man called Norman Ryder. Ryder's an international character who operates under various names. It was Ryder that Winter telephoned. He told him about the diary and said he'd be well advised to get hold of it. Needless to say, Ryder telephoned me.
Mark About the diary?
Howard No; but that's obviously what he had in mind. He simply said he wanted to see me about a book he was writing.
Mark (*at length; smiling*) About a book he was writing ...

Howard stares at Mark, but his manner would appear to be quite friendly

Howard Ryder, don't you think it's about time we discussed the real reason why you came here this evening? If we're going to do a deal over the diary, I suggest we get down to it.

Mark My dear fellow, I agree! I couldn't agree more! But first, I think I'd better bring you up-to-date on this affair. Do you happen to know where your wife is at this precise moment?

Howard My wife? Why, yes! She's with her mother who hasn't been well — or she's on her way home.

Mark You're wrong on both counts. Your wife is being entertained by friends of mine. They picked her up earlier this evening whilst she was waiting for a taxi.

A look of anger appears on Howard's face

Mark (*quietly; yet a distinct threat*) I'm sure, I don't have to remind you of what happened to Winter?

Howard No, you don't have to remind me.

Mark Winter discovered I was Ryder. He promised me he wouldn't talk, but I never take chances — not with the Rex Winters of this world. That's why I was tailing him the day he stole your wife's handbag. I wanted to find out what he was up to. (*A moment; with authority*) Now — so far as your wife's concerned, the situation's simple. Her wellbeing depends on you. Entirely on you. No-one else.

Howard Get to the point, Ryder! You want the diary!

Mark Yes, but not just the diary.

Howard (*puzzled*) Not just the diary?

Mark No. It so happens I'm curious about something. Intensely curious. And you're the only person who can satisfy my curiosity. (*Pause*) According to Winter you had other things belonging to Perry Kingsley. An important letter, photographs, tapes, etc. All of which you handed over to the police.

Howard hesitates, then gives a nod

Why didn't you give them the diary? Why keep the diary back?

Howard I wanted to read it.

Mark But surely you had ample opportunity to read it before you handed it over?

Howard (*a shade aggressively*) I had one reason, and one reason only, for keeping the diary. Perry was blackmailing my wife and I wanted to find out if he'd mentioned her.

Act II, Scene 5

Mark Is she mentioned in the diary?
Howard Yes, she is. There's a reference to her car and what happened at Milton Cross the night you had your meeting with Perry. But here's the diary! Read it! (*He produces the diary and puts it on the desk*)

Mark moves down to the desk and picks the diary up. There is a long pause during which Mark concentrates on the contents of the diary. Finally, he turns towards Howard and is about to say something, when he realizes that Howard is staring at his watch

Mark (*surprised*) Why are you staring at your watch? You consulted it five minutes ago. Are you expecting someone?

Silence

Are you?

Silence

You heard what I said! Are you expecting anyone?
Howard (*quietly*) Yes, I am. (*Pause*) If you must know, I'm expecting my wife.
Mark Your wife! What the devil are you talking about? You know what's happened to your wife! I've told you!

Howard slowly shakes his head

Howard During the past twenty-four hours the police have been keeping a close eye on Joanna. Earlier today they foiled an attempt to abduct her. Your so-called friends have been taken into custody.
Mark I don't believe this! You're bluffing!

Howard indicates the phone

Howard That was the message I received from Inspector Coldwell. It had nothing to do with Rex Winter.
Mark You're lying! I don't believe you!

Nevertheless, Mark is shaken by Howards's statement and he snatches up the phone and starts dialling. There is a pause before we hear the number ringing out at the other end

A long pause

Mark finally realizes that there is going to be no reply and he slams down the receiver

Howard Now perhaps you'll believe me. It's your friends that are being entertained, not my wife.
Mark (*spitting out the words*) You son of a bitch! (*He produces a gun*)

Howard doesn't hesitate. He picks up his drink and throws the whisky straight into Mark's face. Mark instinctively drops the gun on to the desk and covers his eyes. Howard quickly picks up the gun, crosses to the window, and draws back the curtains. Having done this he returns to the desk. The two men once again face each other

   Chris enters from the garden

There is a tense pause

Mark decides to make his escape, rushing across the room towards the hall

   Mark almost reaches the hall when a uniformed police officer springs into the room. He is armed with a Koch MP5 semi-automatic gun. The gun is pointing at Mark

Mark (*hesitating; then with a note of authority*) I wish to make a phone call.
Chris Later!
Mark I know my rights, Inspector, and I demand ——

Chris ignores Mark and nods to the officer. The officer immediately threatens Mark with the Koch and ushers him towards the hall

   Mark and the officer exit

Howard joins Chris

Howard (*anxiously*) Where's Joanna?
Chris Not to worry, sir. She'll be with you in a minute. Let's deal with the tape.

There is the sound of police sirens as Howard starts to take off his jacket

Pause

   Here's your wife now, sir.

Act II, Scene 5

Howard hands Chris the jacket

Howard Take the whole bag of tricks! I shall be glad to get rid of it. It's been very uncomfortable at times.

The police sirens reach their peak, then finally stop

Chris is removing a recording device from the inside of the jacket

Pause

Joanna enters. She looks like a woman who has had an unpleasant experience. Her body appears tense, her face still shows signs of distress

Howard My God, Joanna! How are you? How are you feeling?
Joanna Well – I'm certainly feeling better than I did! Thanks to the Inspector.
Chris (*smiling*) Any time, Mrs Mansfield. (*He puts the sports jacket on a chair*) I'm off, sir. We'll be in touch later.

Chris goes

Howard What actually happened, Joanna? Or would you rather not talk about it?
Joanna I was waiting for a taxi when two men grabbed hold of me and tried to force me into a car. I panicked! Then suddenly – thank God – the police arrived.

For a second or two she appears overwrought and Howard takes hold of her

Pause

Howard You look to me as if you could use a drink.
Joanna No. No, thank you, Howard, not at the moment.
Howard (*releasing her*) Well, I've got some good news for you. It should cheer you up. You can start driving again, that's official.

Joanna has only heard part of what Howard has said

Pause

Joanna What did you say?
Howard I said, you can start driving again. It's official.
Joanna (*forcefully*) I've no intention of driving again — ever!

The Curtain *falls*

FURNITURE AND PROPERTY LIST

ACT I

Scene 1

On stage: Collection of books and pictures. Painting titled "Flowers On a Tray", photograph depicting **Joanna** with **Grace**
Armchairs
Tables
Comfortable sofa
Drinks cabinet. *In it*: glasses, drinks including a bottle of Scotch
Several occasional pieces
Curtains
Desk with drawers and a built-in cupboard. *On it*: telephone, large stiletto type letter opener, various letters.
Breakfast table and two chairs. *On table*: books, manuscripts (etc.)

Off stage: Bulky-looking manuscript (**Grace**)
Large, expensive-looking handbag. *In it*: wallet, bunch of keys, credit cards, bank statement, personal alarm resembling a small torch (**Grace**)
Dress-shop carrier (**Mark**)

Personal: **Howard**: watch (worn throughout)
Mark: watch (worn throughout)

Scene 2

On stage: As Scene 1

Off stage: Tiny bottle of red nail polish (**Joanna**)
Rug (**Joanna**)
Pair of gloves (**Howard**)

Personal: **Perry**: squat .44 magnum gun

Furniture and Property List

Scene 3

Set: Bottle of red nail polish on table

Scene 4

Set: Window open

Off stage: Valise (**Chris**)

Scene 5

On stage: As Scene 1

Off stage: Books (**Howard**)

ACT II

Scene 1

On stage: As ACT I, Scene 1

During black-out page 41

Strike: Books etc. from breakfast table

Set: Drink, cigarette and ashtray on breakfast table

During black-out page 42

Strike: Drink, ashtray

Set: Books on breakfast table

Off stage: Newspaper (**Mark**)

Personal: **Chris**: envelope with notes on the back

Scene 2

On stage: As ACT I, Scene 1

Re-set: Garden window open

Off stage:　　Painting — "Flowers On A Tray" (**Chris**)
　　　　　　　Briefcase containing several large photographs, airmail letter, diary (**Grace**)
　　　　　　　Night-dress, make-up box, dressing-gown (**Joanna**)

Scene 3

On stage:　　As previous scene

Personal:　　**Chris**: wallet containing card with writing on it

Scene 4

Set:　　　　Large envelope containing photographs for **Howard**
　　　　　　　Photographs, replica of **Perry**'s diary in desk drawer
Check:　　　Garden window open

Scene 5

On stage:　　As previous scene

Off stage:　　Koch MP5 semi-automatic gun (**Policeman**)

Personal:　　**Mark**: gun
　　　　　　　Chris: recording device

Samuel French is grateful to Charles Vance, Vice-Chairman of the Theatres Advisory Council, for the following information regarding the Firearms (Amendment) Bill:

"The Firearms (Amendment) Bill does not affect blank-firing pistols which are not readily convertible (i.e. those which do not require a Firearms Certificate). Among the reasons against imposing restrictions on such items is their use in theatre, cinema and television as a "safe" alternative to real guns."

"The general prohibition on the possession of real handguns will apply to those used for theatrical purposes. It would clearly be anomalous to prohibit the use of those items for target shooting, but permit their use for purposes where a fully-working gun is not needed. As handguns will become "Section 5" prohibited weapons, they would fall under the same arrangements as at present apply to real machine guns. As you will know, there are companies which are authorised by the Secretary of State to supply such weapons for theatrical purposes."

The exemption under Section 12 of the Firearms Act 1968, whereby actors can use firearms without themselves having a Firearms Certificate, will remain in force.

Regulations apply to the United Kingdom only. Producers in other countries should refer to appropriate legislation.

LIGHTING PLOT

ACT I, SCENE 1. Afternoon, July

To open: Bright interior lighting; afternoon light through window

Cue 1: **Joanna** rushes out of the room (Page 15)
Fade to black-out

ACT I, SCENE 2. Later the same day

To open: General interior lighting. Dim light through window

Cue 2: **Howard**: " ... in Holland Park." (Page 21)
Black-out

ACT I, SCENE 3. Three hours later

To open: General interior lighting

Cue 3: **Howard** looks at the bottle of varnish (Page 26)
Fade to black-out

ACT I, SCENE 4. The next morning

To open: Bright interior lighting; sunshine through open window

Cue 4: **Chris** exits (Page 32)
Fade quickly to black-out

ACT I, SCENE 5. Early evening

To open: General interior lighting

Cue 5: **Howard**: " *Was he?*" (Page 37)
Fade quickly to black-out

ACT II, SCENE 1. The same day. Early evening

To open: General interior lighting

Cue 6:	**Joanna**: "Eventually ..." *Fade to black-out*	(Page 40)
Cue 7:	**Joanna** sits at breakfast table in alcove. When ready *Bring lights up on alcove*	(Page 40)
Cue 8:	**Perry**: " ... bad at the moment." *The lights start to fade*	(Page 41)
Cue 9:	**Perry**: " ...London in the Merc." *Fade to black-out*	(Page 41)
Cue 10:	**Perry** exits. When ready *General interior lights gradually rise to reveal* **Joanna** *and* **Howard**	(Page 42)
Cue 11:	**Chris**: "... as soon as possible." *The lights start to fade*	(Page 49)
Cue 12:	**Chris** exits *Black-out*	(Page 49)

ACT II, SCENE 2. Two hours later

To open: General interior lighting. Light to suggest evening through open window

Cue 13:	**Howard**: " ... about half an hour ago." *Black-out*	(Page 61)

ACT II, SCENE 3. One hour later

To open: General interior lighting. Light to suggest evening through open window

Cue 14:	**Chris**: " ... in about an hour." *The lights fade*	(Page 66)

ACT II, SCENE 4. The following morning

To open: Sunny interior lighting. Light through open window

Cue 15:	**Rex** falls into **Howard**'s arms. Pause *Black-out*	(Page 72)

ACT II, SCENE 5. Several hours later

To open: General interior lighting

No cues

EFFECTS PLOT

ACT I

Cue 1:	**Hilary**: " You did warn me." *The doorbell rings*	(Page 2)
Cue 2:	**Howard** looks at the bank statement *The doorbell rings loud and unexpected*	(Page 7)
Cue 3:	**Howard** freezes. Pause. *The doorbell rings and continues until door is answered*	(Page 7)
Cue 4:	**Howard** turns away from **Joanna** *The telephone rings*	(Page 15)
Cue 5:	**Howard** nods and is about to comment *The telephone rings*	(Page 25)
Cue 6:	**Howard**: " ... difficult to tell on the phone" *The doorbell rings and continues until ready*	(Page 28)

ACT II

Cue 7:	**Joanna**: " He must be." *The doorbell rings*	(Page 43)
Cue 8:	**Howard**: " ... know what they say." *The telephone rings*	(Page 45)
Cue 9:	**Howard** laughs *The doorbell rings*	(Page 50)
Cue 10:	**Hilary**: " ... must have been." *The doorbell rings*	(Page 54)
Cue 11:	**Howard** crosses to the desk and puts the diary down *The telephone rings*	(Page 60)
Cue 12:	To open Scene 3 *The telephone rings*	(Page 61)

Cue 13:	**Howard** picks up the phone *The doorbell rings*	(Page 61)
Cue 14:	**Howard**: "... such a bad idea." *The doorbell rings*	(Page 67)
Cue 15:	**Mark**: " Thank you." *The telephone rings*	(Page 72)
Cue 16:	**Mark** dials a number. Pause *The number rings out the other end*	(Page 75)
Cue 17:	**Chris**: "Let's deal with the tape." *Sound of police car sirens in the distance; getting nearer*	(Page 76)
Cue 18:	**Howard**: " ... been very uncomfortable at times" *Police car sirens reach their peak, then stop*	(Page 77)